Praise for *Blessed Union*

"Sarah Griffith Lund's groundbreaking book on mental Illness and marriage boldly bears witness to the all too often silenced and shame-inducing experiences of marriages impacted by mental illness in ways that are radically restorative. If you or someone you love needs to be reminded of how both blessed and sacred unions impacted by mental illness really are, this book is a must read."–**Christina Davis, Clinical Assistant Professor of Pastoral Theology and Marriage and Family Therapy, Christian Theological Seminary**

"Lund offers story after story of marriages with mental illness and integrates them with the most well-known ideas and scriptures about marriage. In so doing, she pushes us to reconsider, adapt, and nourish the ways that mental illness impacts deep loving relationships. This is a must-read book for clergy, pre-marital counselors, married folk, those of us who know we live with mental health challenges and those of us who don't."–**Monica A. Coleman, author, *Bipolar Faith: A Black Woman's Journey with Depression and Faith***

"This one-of-a-kind book invites the reader into the most intimate relationship—marriage, and the most challenging illness—mental illness. Sarah offers hope and help to couples with mental health challenges, reminding all of us that God's love never ends."–**Hollie M. Holt-Woehl, Adjunct Professor, Luther Seminary**

"Through stories and honest theological reflection, Sarah offers us a revised practical theology of love and marriage that will help all of us to love more fully even in the midst of the most difficult of circumstances."–**John Swinton, Professor in Practical Theology and Pastoral Care, University of Aberdeen, Scotland, United Kingdom**

"Interweaving scripture, personal stories, and education, *Blessed Union* offers an honest, nuanced look into the realities of mental illness and their effects on intimate partnerships. Organized with reflection questions, specific diagnostic criteria, and tips for self-care, *Blessed Union* is a useful guide for individuals and support-groups, as well as a resource for training pastoral care teams on mental illness and its effects."–**Sonia Waters, Associate Professor of Pastoral Theology, Princeton Theological Seminary**

"Through the intimate stories of couples living with mental illness in their marriage, Lund helps to break the stigma around this urgent topic. Lund invites us to come alongside people living with mental health challenges and to find hope in supportive community."—**Leah Gunning Francis, Vice-President for Academic Affairs at Christian Theological Seminary and author of Ferguson and Faith: Sparking Leadership and Awakening Community**

"*Blessed Union* is a must read for all pastors. The very poignant glimpses into different marriages serves to remind us all how mental illness can be painfully destructive in any relationship. Helping couples navigate mental health crises or continuing symptoms of mental illness is sacred work the church would do well to engage in.—**Rachel Keefe, pastor and author of *The Lifesaving Church: Faith Communities and Suicide Prevention***

"This dynamic and rich compilation of heartwarming and heart-wrenching stories of the author and brave couples shows how the power of love can break through the shadow of darkness cast by the stigma and shame of mental illness and addiction. Through reflections, questions, tips, and prayers, Lund equips the reader to break the silence and embrace their blessed union by holding fast to the 'Big Blessed Love' that is forever."–**Jermine D. Alberty, Executive Director, Pathways to Promise**

"This book is a vital contribution to the growing conversation about faithful living in the midst of mental health challenges." – **David Finnegan-Hosey, author of *Christ on the Psych Ward* and *Grace is a Pre-Existing Condition: Faith, Systems, and Mental Healthcare***

"*Blessed Union* proclaims that absolutely nothing, not even mental illness and its impact on marital relationships, can ever separate us from God and God's unconditional love. The prayers and invitations to journaling encourage spiritual practice and theological reflection on mental health, marriage, and God's presence in the midst of it all."–**Adam Hanley, Program Coordinator for Ministry Personnel Vitality, The United Church of Canada**

"This comprehensive book weaves together spiritual insights, psychological understandings, wisdom of good marriage therapists, biblical supports, and a welcomed internal exploration to be real in our own marriages. While breaking the silence about mental illness in marriages can be painful, it is even more painful to stay silent."–**Alan Johnson, United Church of Christ clergy and founder of the Interfaith Network on Mental Illness**

"Sarah's work is the perfect balance of research, science, faith, stories, seriousness, and humor. The reflection questions are poignant and perfect for couples or small groups to study and reflect together. As a pastor who longs to offer resources to people searching for help, I am so grateful for this gift that I can share with couples who desire to strengthen their marriages."–**Mark P. Briley, Lead Minister, Broadway Christian Church (Disciples of Christ), Columbia, Missouri**

Blessed Union

Breaking the Silence about
Mental Illness and Marriage

Sarah Griffith Lund

chalice
press

Saint Louis, Missouri

ChalicePress.com

Print: 9780827203143
EPUB: 9780827203150
EPDF: 9780827203167

Printed in the United States of America

Contents

For everyone living with mental illness and the people who love us.

In memory of my maternal grandmother
Beulah Mae Wilson
(January 19, 1921—May 16, 2020)

You are altogether beautiful, my darling,
beautiful in every way.

—Song of Songs 4:7, (NIV)

Perhaps it is good to have a beautiful mind,
but an even greater gift is to discover a
beautiful heart.

—Sylvia Nasar, *A Beautiful Mind*

Breaking the Silence

We don't tell the stories we most need to hear. We tell the stories we want other people to hear. It makes telling true stories hard. It makes telling true stories radical.

This is the true, hard, and radical story about the ways mental illness and mental health challenges show up in our most intimate relationships: our marriages or committed partnerships, also known in religious language as our blessed unions.

Blessed unions represent the deepest level of commitment, faithfulness, companionship, and love. Blessed unions come about because of the desire of our hearts to fully know the other and to be fully known by the other. Blessed unions are sacred because within the union we are invited to experience the loving gaze of God. In our blessed unions, we pledge to love, honor, cherish, respect, support, and grow alongside our partner.

Within the blessed union we discover who we are, who we can be, who we don't want to be, and who we don't want to become. Within the blessed union we can flourish, and we can fall. It is in this intimate partnership where we see ourselves in the full-length mirror, the mirror that surrounds us on all sides, and we begin to see parts of ourselves we did not know were there. We see our shadow sides, we see the back side, and we see the parts of us we work so hard to hide from ourselves and from others.

This book explores the topic of mental illness and marriage through the telling of true stories, including my own. We will specifically be looking at the impact of addiction, anxiety, autism spectrum disorder, bipolar disorder, depression, eating disorders, hoarding disorder, obsessive-compulsive disorder, postpartum depression, posttraumatic stress disorder, schizophrenia, suicidality, and unspecified psychotic disorder. That's enough for now. If you don't see a mental health condition that reflects your own experience included on this list, please accept my apologies. I hope that you get to share your story, too. We need to hear everyone's stories, and this is just a start.

The stories told here represent a collection of stories inspired by couples and were collected over a period of a few years. Though I have pastored several churches, not all the stories are based on parishioners or professional colleagues of mine. In some cases, I have gathered details from various couples and put them into the same story. The names and the identifying details of the couples are altered while the truths of the stories are preserved. In every case I have told the truth to the best of my ability. As they say on the acclaimed storytelling podcast, *The Moth*: "stories are true as remembered and affirmed by the storyteller."

Starting in 2014, as I met with people across the country in churches from Oakland, California, to Des Moines, Iowa, to Miami, Florida, to Lancaster, Pennsylvania, discussing my first book *Blessed Are the Crazy: Breaking the Silence About Mental Illness, Family and Church*, I asked people if there was interest in exploring the topic of mental health and marriages. Their affirmations and encouragement led me here to you now and to this book inspired by marriage partners living with mental illness. This book is my response to the deep longing for this conversation and I am honored to contribute a small part to this ongoing work of breaking the silence about mental illness.

I include religious leaders, such as pastors and chaplains, among the individuals whose stories I share, because the stigma of mental illness is particularly strong for religious leaders, who tend to get placed on a pedestal. These stories are told through my own lens as a highly educated, middle-class, European-American, heterosexual, and cisgender married woman and mother. I write this book as a person in recovery from a mental health condition and as the spouse of a person who is also in recovery from mental health conditions.

In this book I am writing through the lens of mental health and disabilities justice, which has informed my pastoral work for many years. In both my professional and personal experience, it's become clear to me that ableism impacts our understanding of what makes a healthy marriage. Ableism is society's assumption that able-bodied (bodies without disabilities) and neuro-typical (brains without mental illness) people are better than people living with disabilities and mental health challenges.

Ableism fuels discrimination, stigma, and inequality for people with disabilities and mental health challenges. In society at large, ableism creates barriers to affordable and accessible healthcare. In the field of faith and marriage, ableism assumes marriages exist among people without disabilities and mental health challenges. Ableism silences the stories we need to hear. Ableism silences our stories. This book breaks the silence about mental illness and marriage.

Since this is not a collection of scientifically oriented case studies, but a collection of stories, I've chosen to focus on the dynamic at play between mental illness and its impact on a marriage covenant. To be sure, future work needs to be done to explore various intersectionalities: race and mental illness; poverty and mental illness; education level, age, physical disabilities, and gender identity. All our multiple identities have bearing on how we experience mental illness and what resources we have access to for healing. However, my primary purpose here is to provide a starting point for conversations about mental illness and marriage, trusting others will add their voices as time goes on. Breaking the silence about mental illness is something each one of us can do. Each story and each voice is important. Including yours.

Mental Illness Defined

First, let's be clear that mental illness is a physical illness. Even though it is often invisible, it is very much real and not just "all in my head." Simply stated, mental illness can be understood as a health condition affecting a person's thinking, feeling, personality, behavior, judgment, perception, and mood. Mental illness impacts all our relationships, especially our intimate relationships, because mental illness affects our ability to relate to others and our ability to function on a daily basis.

Mental illness is a medical condition, just like heart disease or diabetes. Our mental health exists on a spectrum over the course of our lifetime. Mental illness can be experienced at many levels from mild to severe. It is important to know that mental illness is treatable, though some people may need medical care, including hospitalization.

Mental illness can occur at any time in our life, with symptoms appearing across the span of a person's life, from newborns to old age, and every age in between. Mental illness does not discriminate based on religion, sex, age, gender, race, culture, nationality, income, or ability. Mental illness can happen to anyone.

We don't yet know exactly what causes mental illness, but we do know several factors are at play. Mental illness can be caused and influenced by a combination of biology, genetics, environment, situations, history, and unknown influences. As noted above, we all are at risk for developing mental illness at any stage in life, though most serious mental illnesses emerge by early adulthood.

Some of the most tearful and emotional stories I've heard are from mothers of young adults who develop serious mental illness their freshman year of college. Fifty percent of all lifetime cases of mental illness begin by the age of fourteen and three quarters of them begin by the age of twenty-four, according to the National Institute of Mental Health (NIMH). This means that teenagers and young adults are experiencing life-altering changes in their mental health status, often with very little support in place.

Even with the best intentions for taking good care of our health—and despite protective factors such as access to resources that support healthy lifestyles (exercise, healthy food, leisure activities, and rest)—people can still get sick. Because of the influence of genetics, children of parents with depression are two to four times more likely to develop depression, according to the Anxiety and Depression Association of America. Currently there is no known cure for serious mental illnesses such as bipolar disorder or schizophrenia, though most people can experience reduced symptoms and better quality of life with medication and therapy. Recovery, that is, feeling better while managing and coping with the illness, is possible.

According to a special edition of TIME magazine on mental health from July of 2019, depression ranks among the most common causes of disability in the US. Unlike polio and other illnesses that disable us or cause premature death, there's no immunization for mental illness. It shows up in human populations around the world and is a common part of human experience. To be human is to experience the full spectrum of mental health. Mental illness is not a character flaw, weakness, sin, punishment from God, or moral failure.

Since mental illness is a physical, biological medical health condition, that means anyone with a body and a brain can get sick. Just as there are protective factors, however, there are risk factors too. According to the World Health Organization:

> Mental health and mental illnesses are determined by multiple and interacting social, psychological and biological factors, just as health and illness in general. The clearest evidence for this relates to the risk of mental illnesses, which in the developed and developing world is associated with indicators of poverty, including low levels of education, and in some

studies with poor housing and low income. The greater vulnerability of disadvantaged people in each community to mental illnesses may be explained by such factors as the experience of insecurity and hopelessness, rapid social change, and the risks of violence and physical ill-health.[1]

Even with the advances in knowledge and with growing public awareness of mental illness over the past decade, there remains significant stigma surrounding mental illness. Many people hold misperceptions about whether mental illnesses are treatable or whether learning healthy habits can help aid recovery (the answers are yes, and yes!). Some worry about losing their jobs or being perceived as a credit risk, or being perceived as violent, if they disclose they are taking medications or receiving therapy for mental illnesses.[2]

Just as we have integrated sex education into the health and science curriculum in our public schools (and into some of our Christian education programs too), we need to have mental health education for children and young people. The sooner we teach our children about mental health, the better prepared they will be to care for themselves or others who experience mental illness. Focusing on prevention early will help reduce the severity of mental illness later in life. If we know the signs and symptoms of mental illness, then we can surround our young people with support and resources to encourage mental wellness.

Typically, we think of mental illness as either depression or anxiety, or as serious mental illnesses such as bipolar or schizophrenia. Yet, there are as many as 300 different specific types of mental health conditions outlined in *The Diagnostic and Statistical Manual of Mental Disorders, Fifth Edition (DSM-5)*, a reference source compiled with input from hundreds of international researchers and practitioners from all fields of mental health. We continue to discover more and more about the brain every day. However, for most forms of mental illness there remains no easy cure.

It's never a good idea to try to diagnose yourself or other people unless you are a trained mental health professional. It's an easy trap to fall into. How often have you heard someone say, "she's acting schizophrenic"? Labeling someone as a person with a mental illness who has not already described themselves that way, or disclosed to you their diagnosis, increases the stigma and can be used to shame them. If you think someone needs help, the best thing to do is to listen with compassion and connect them to a mental health professional (see *Resources* section, pg. 147).

Do not try to treat serious mental illness yourself. Self-medicating with alcohol and drugs is a common way for people to numb themselves to the pain of mental illness. Unfortunately, this can lead to addiction and cause further suffering. Remember that mental illness is a physical medical condition and requires professional attention.

The Myth of Perfect Love

It is especially hard to tell the true stories of imperfect love. The myth of perfect romantic love is pervasive in our culture, and we feel like failures when our marriages fall short. We don't want to talk about our failures, imperfections, and shortfalls, especially when it comes to love.

Nobody likes to fail. But perhaps the most painful of all failures is failing at love. For many Christians, we believe God is at the center of our marriages. We include scripture and prayer in our wedding ceremonies. A priest or a minister officiates our weddings.

As people of faith we believe that God's presence in our journey together somehow gives us an extra layer of protection over and above what the law affords us. Therefore, failing at love may mean, for some of us, we have also failed God. Or worse, God has failed us, abandoned us, and divorced us.

According to Johns Hopkins Medicine, one in four of us will experience a diagnosable mental illness in any given year. Given this, it is possible as many as one in five couples will experience life together with mental illness as part of the equation. Since mental illness impacts the mind, body, and soul, how does mental illness impact the ability to give and receive love in the context of holy marriage? Can people with mental illness still live happily ever after?

Through our explorations in this book, my goal is to find hope for healing when we tell these stories about love and loss, about flourishing and failing, about marriage and mental illness. My hope is that you will take heart knowing you are not alone. My prayer is that in these words you find community, comfort, and compassion for yourself.

When happiness is hard to come by, we often blame ourselves. Mental illness is not your fault. You are trying your best. I hope here in this book you will find some tools to help you along the way.

Breaking the silence about mental illness and holy marriage is a countercultural and radical act. It's countercultural not only because it pierces the mythology of perfect love but because it confronts the stigma and shame that exists within society, especially in the church, towards mental illness. When we can speak openly, honestly, respectfully, and compassionately about pain and doubt in our most intimate relationships, we help to restore dignity and humanity for people living with mental illness and our loved ones. To tell the true story is to heal our hearts that have been broken by the pain of mental illness.

What stories do we tell about marriage? In fairy tales, such as *Cinderella*, marriage is the way to live happily ever after. Times haven't changed much. Still today, the main reason people get married is to be happy. Why is happiness in marriage so hard sometimes?

I did some research to find out. In my reading, I discovered that books about marriage often do not consider the additional challenges of mental illness when it comes to finding happiness in the marriage. Finding happiness in a "normal" marriage untouched by mental illness is one thing—and hard enough already. Adding mental health challenges in one or both people in the marriage, on top of everyday annoyances and hardships, launches the marriage into a new galaxy. We need to tell the stories of these kind of marriages, too.

Let's pretend you are a person without a mental illness. Then most marriage books are for you. For example, *The Happy Couple* by Barton Goldsmith outlines key techniques couples can apply to their marriages to find happiness. Readers need only apply patience and persistence to replace habits that are bad for the relationship with good ones. For example: practice finding humor in everyday situations like washing dishes; learn to say you're sorry. Yet, for marriages like mine where there is mental illness, finding happiness is not as simple as changing a bad behavior or annoying habit. The trouble with applying these techniques to marriages with mental illness is that the change needed for happiness may go deeper than behavior; it can involve changing brain chemistry as well.

Yes, people in blessed unions with mental illness want to be happy couples like everyone else, but it's not as simple or easy as books for the general public make it sound. It doesn't take five keys to find happiness, but 5,000 keys when there is mental illness in the marriage.

For example, according to *The Happy Couple*, the most important part of a happy marriage is communication. I do not disagree, but in marriages with mental illness, often the couple's communication abilities are most acutely impacted by symptoms of depression and anxiety.

In my own marriage, mental illness is annoying and frustrating. Mental illness gets in the way of communication. When a depressive episode moves in, the communication moves out. Once while sitting with our marriage therapist, I asked my husband what a wellness plan would look like for our marriage. I wanted to have a plan we both agreed on for when a depressive episode begins. He said, "The best thing you can do is to leave me alone." While that is clear communication, it also is a dead end.

My own experience of being in recovery from posttraumatic stress disorder means that when I come to a relational dead end, I either freeze, fight, or flee. The challenge for my partner and me is how to stay emotionally connected and in relationship when we can't talk to each other. Depressive episodes happen with regularity in our marriage, so I am learning how to honor his desire to be left alone during these times. I am also learning how to stay present and not detach when my own childhood fears of neglect or abandonment surface.

How do you build a happy marriage when chronic mental illness causes regular periods of no communication or interaction? Several of the key recommendations for a happy marriage in *The Happy Couple* and similar advice books are, in fact, habits mental illness makes very difficult, if not nearly impossible: communication, gratitude, humor, acknowledgement, interdependence, celebration, playfulness, meeting needs, acceptance, positivity, connection, honesty, nurturing, balance, togetherness, problem solving, affection, compassion, thoughtfulness, respectful arguing, security, enjoyment, and emotional development.

The Happy Couple ends with a pep talk to readers: "at some point in our lives, we all must confront our bad habits. When it comes to the habits we manifest in our relationships, confronting them can be more challenging but it's worth it. It's time for you to confront your own bad habits and turn them around. You can do it" (pg. 178).

But is mental illness simply a bad habit that we can turn around? How do we distinguish between bad habits and mental illness? Can we find happiness in the same way as everyone else? Or do we need a different way? This book is about exploring a different way to be in a blessed union with mental illness. Mental illness is not a bad habit that can be un-learned, reshaped, or pep talked away. We need another way.

Talking about how mental illness affects marriage is indeed countercultural. It is also an act of restorative justice. Restorative justice is not simply about punishing wrongs; it is also concerned with repairing harm caused by wrongdoing.

Restorative justice is a theme in God's relationships with human communities in the Bible. Recognizing this as part of our religious heritage, we—I, other Christian leaders, and you who read this book as part of your faith journey—wish for the restoration to wholeness and the ability to participate fully in God's kingdom for individuals, and for relationships, broken by mental illness. Mental illness, understood as a disease (the same way we understand cancer, for example), can cause us and our relationships harm. Diseases themselves aren't caused by any individual's wrongdoing, but the fact that they cause harm to our bodies and throw our relationships off balance does, in part, have its roots in human, systemic, wrongdoing.

More than acceptance, we want justice for all who experience mental illness in their blessed unions. To help you see the love stories I'm about to share through a lens of justice, I offer in Chapter One some background about social and restorative justice traditions in the church as they relate specifically to mental illness. People with mental illness are often discriminated against, shamed, and silenced. Telling our stories about mental illness and marriage is a liberating act of love and justice.

In these pages, I hope to reassure you, if you or your intimate partner has mental illness, or if both of you do, you are not alone. This book is also helpful if someone you care about—a friend, adult child, sibling, neighbor, church member, or co-worker—is in a marriage where there is mental illness. Feeling emotionally distant, isolated, and afraid are all too common in marriages struggling to find mental balance. Together, we can break the silence about mental illness in the blessed union.

Mental illness can steal the joy from marriage. We may worry there is no hope and our marriage is doomed. But it is possible to find a way through. Our worst moments do not last forever. Through the shadows of mental illness, we look for the rays of light. We find light for our journey by breaking the silence that isolates and shames us and keeps us feeling alone in the shadows. This book shines a light, showing us a way forward.

Marriages with mental illness can flourish. With the right combination of support, painfully honest conversations, a willingness to work towards recovery and symptom management, and a commitment to sticking together through the hard parts, we can joyfully receive God's blessing on our unions. Even with mental illness in the mix, our unions can be blessed indeed—not just bearable, but life-affirming. We, too, can live happily ever after. It just might look a little different and we might need to take a different path. We can create the way forward together.

Never Alone

There may come a time in any marriage when the best course of action is to end the marriage. Divorce is painful, expensive, inconvenient, and in some cases the right thing to do. There can be tremendous guilt for wanting a divorce when our partner is living with a chronic illness, such as bipolar disorder or an eating disorder. We may wonder if we are horrible people for reaching a point in the marriage where we cannot go on. There is still shame and stigma associated with divorce, especially in some religious communities.

For some, divorce is the way to live happily ever after. I've witnessed the joy in my own family members and friends who find happiness in life after a divorce. It may take a divorce for both individuals to discover health and wellness. While we seek to honor our marriage vows, not every marriage honors us. When a marriage chronically harms us, we need to take steps to be free.

My family personally knows the deep pain and serious harm an unhealthy marriage can cause. Recently, I asked my mother to share with me about her own marriage journey with mental illness since my father lived with chronic, severe, and untreated mental illness. I learned that my mother never believed in divorce, even when her marriage counselor looked her straight in the eyes and said, "Can't you see that somebody is going to get killed? If you have any place on this Earth you can go, you better go there now." After years of psychotic episodes, my father's behavior crossed a line when he ran over my oldest brother with his truck in our driveway after school. Despite my father's abusive behavior, my mother still couldn't bring herself to divorce him since nobody in her family got divorced and her religion taught against it.

Today, I am grateful to my mother for saving our lives by leaving my father and taking us to live with our grandparents who lived on the other side of the country from our father. Still, she says she didn't want a divorce. She wanted to keep her marriage vows and she said she would do whatever it took to make her marriage work. It wasn't until my father started kidnapping us that she went from separation to seeking legal divorce. When one of us went missing, the sheriff would say our father had the legal right to take us. In the end, divorce was the only way my mother could protect us children from the negative direct impact of our father's severe, untreated mental illness. My mother found out there are times when divorce is the only option if you want to survive.

It could be that marriage makes the symptoms of mental illness worse. Seeking professional support from qualified marriage counselors can help you to discern if the marriage is going to be a pathway for healing. Marriages with mental illness do not have to end in divorce, but many do because it is the healthier decision for both partners. Divorce can be a pathway to new life.

But how do we figure out which path to be on? The pathway of marriage with mental illness or the pathway of divorce? The real struggle may be in discerning the path forward, one day at a time. Sometimes there is no clear way forward. The good news is, we don't have to travel this path alone. God is with us as we walk down the aisle toward the altar on our wedding day and God is with us as we walk down roads of uncertainty and confusion.

Chapter One:

Mental Health Justice in the Blessed Union

There is no love without justice. When it comes to matters of faith, justice is an important ingredient in God's love. Justice ensures equal access to opportunities to flourish as children of God—in other words, to be happy. Biblical justice happens in our relationships with one another, too. Biblical characteristics of justice are fairness, generosity, and equity.

A key Bible verse that shapes my own ministry is Micah 6:8, "What does the Lord require of you but to do justice, and to love kindness, and to walk humbly with your God?" Doing justice on a personal and relational level means building right relationships that show respect and honor and value the worth of each person as a beloved child of God. With this strong foundation, we can begin to build relationships that embody justice. Our blessed unions can reflect God's loving justice in our lives and be the place from which we grow in the image of a loving God.

Marriages that are loving are also just. Not too many wedding ceremonies include a reading from Micah 6:8, but what happens when justice is a missing ingredient in marital love? When our marriages lack respect, honor, and equality, then it may not be love that is life-giving.

We don't often associate marriage with justice, but what if we did? Justice in marriage means being in life-giving relationships in which partners mutually bless each other. How does the injustice of mental illness impact a marriage? When mental illness becomes a burden without the sense of blessing, there can be a sense of inequality in the relationship and a lack of justice.

Mental illness creates injustice in the marriage when it robs us of our sense of value and dignity. This dynamic causes tension within relationships because feeling like a burden lowers our self-esteem and sense of self-worth. How can we fully honor and value others when we don't honor and value ourselves as equals? The injustice of mental illness is that it can distort our sense of worthiness. Mental illness lies about who is worthy and who is not.

If a person with mental illness already feels insecure and worthless because of their mental illness, then the justice issue is the lack of value of the self as a child of God. The mental illness violates our sense of well-being and this violation is an injustice. For couples, the injustice runs deep, impacting each person differently.

Thinking about marriage through the lens of justice helps us understand why conversations about health and illness are so important—they affect the balance of a relationship. And it is important to note, justice within a marriage doesn't begin on the wedding day. We can start talking to our children now about how they live out and experience justice in their relationships with friends, and eventually their chosen partners.

Faith communities can instill values of equality, respect, dignity, and self-worth early on. Teaching our children at a young age about just and healthy relationships will help ensure their future flourishing. Honoring ourselves as created in the image of God is foundational to understanding restorative justice in our relationships.

Because each one of us is created in the image of God, no matter our disability or mental illness, we are created good. Our disability and our mental illness do not make us bad people; we are not damaged goods. All people, no matter their disability status or mental health status, are worthy of love, equality, respect, dignity and are of infinite worth.

Mental Health as a Social Justice Issue

Mental health is the foundation for thinking, communication, learning, resilience, and self-esteem. Positive mental health is key to personal, interpersonal, and societal well-being. We rely on our mental health to navigate relationships and contribute to society. Mental health is defined by the World Health Organization as "a state of well-being in which the individual realizes [their] own abilities, can cope with the normal stresses of life, can work productively and fruitfully, and is able to make a contribution to his or her community".[3]

Now, let's take this faith-based concept of justice and apply it to mental health on a societal level. Mental health is a social justice issue because people with mental illness often experience discrimination, stigma, or a lack of accessible and quality mental health resources. Our jails and prisons are filled with people who are penalized for their mental illness. Having a criminal record unfairly punishes people who live with mental illness, making it doubly hard for them to find employment upon their release from prison. This, in turn, causes them to also experience higher levels of poverty than if they'd received treatment, and makes it hard or impossible to access care, completing the vicious cycle. The criminalization of mental illness is another example of ableism in society.

We can think about stigma in at least two different ways: public and self. Public stigma is how the general public views mental illness, which is typically with negative biases, stereotypes, prejudice, and discrimination. One way we perpetuate public stigma is by covering up the truth with silence.

For example, there is the persistent but inaccurate belief that a person with a mental illness is more likely to be violent. The truth is that people living with a mental illness are more likely to be victims of violence than to perpetrate violence onto others. Extensive surveys of police incident reports demonstrate that, far from posing threats to others, people diagnosed with schizophrenia, for example, have victimization rates 65% to 130% higher than those of the general public.[4]

In my family, people own guns and it's a part of the Midwestern culture I grew up in. Guns can be problematic for people with mental illness, though, and not because people with mental illness are more likely than others to commit homicide, but because statistically, they are at a greater risk of harming themselves. Tragically, the most fatal engagements with suicidal behavior include the use of guns.

We know too well by now that when there is a public shooting, the assumption, especially if the shooter is a white male, is that mental illness caused the violence. Yet a database tracking gun homicides, the National Center for Health Statistics, reports less than 5% of gun-related killings in the United States between 2001 and 2010 were perpetrated by people diagnosed with mental illness.[5]

Stigma fuels discrimination against people with mental illness, and the assumption that people with mental illness are a danger to society. Then there is the assumption that people living with a mental illness are somehow broken or fragile, and not capable of flourishing. Our public narrative about mental illness is loaded with stigma and this makes talking about mental illness, especially with regard to oneself or a loved one, difficult because we fear being judged.

Self-stigmatization is prejudice people turn against themselves. For example, when my friend Carrie is experiencing an episode of mental illness, she cannot fulfill her responsibilities at work or with her family. She feels ashamed and inadequate. Carrie feels as if she has let people down and disappointed others. Internalizing the stigma keeps people silent about their own suffering, perpetuating their feelings of shame.

Self-stigma also keeps people from seeking much-needed support. When Carrie was talking with me, she was upset with herself for being sick and blamed herself for her mental illness. I asked if she wanted to share about her current episode with our other friends. "No," she said. "I'm too ashamed."

Many people don't want to talk about mental illness because they are fearful about their own illness and the way it impacts their lives. Self-stigma often leads to low quality of life, creating enormous pain for persons with mental illness. Self-stigma impacts the ability to work, and to support oneself and one's family. This makes it feel like we are not making a positive contribution to society.

The reasons for silence in the face of stigma are understandable in a way. Yet silence perpetuates the stigma and shame. Stigma and shame, in turn, keep us silent. Even when we are committed to telling true stories of our lives, we still edit out the uncomfortable details of mental illness.

For example, in a side conversation at a dinner party, Jennifer, a religious scholar who had recently published a memoir, told me she left out of her story the fact that her partner's untreated mental illness led to their divorce. Thinking back through her book, I realized yes, she did keep silent about mental illness in her marriage. I wondered why she did not include this fact in what was otherwise a very detailed account of her life, so I asked her. Jennifer said, "I just didn't feel comfortable writing about it."

Indeed, she might not have had permission from her ex to do so. Digging a little, I learned her partner had been a university professor. So, might she also have omitted part of her story because of the stigma of mental illness in the academy, where the productivity of the mind is so highly prized?

The cycle of stigma continues until someone speaks up and breaks the silence. Jennifer said she was glad I was writing this book about mental illness and marriage because she couldn't find much support. It is my hope that this book helps create circles of support.

According to the National Alliance on Mental Illness (NAMI), in the US it commonly takes an average of seven years from onset of symptoms to the time a person gets access to treatment. I wondered about Jennifer's marriage and how stigma and shame may have created barriers to support, care, and treatment for recovery and wellness.

In addition to stigma, availability and cost of treatment are justice issues. As I alluded to above, many people in need of treatment cannot afford it and often treatment options are not available, with many communities lacking enough beds, therapists, and other resources.

The problem of lack of resources is exacerbated when we look at communities of color, as systemic racism contributes to the mental health crisis. Historical trauma negatively impacts the mental health of Black communities. Generations of racism and injustice create significant challenges for mental wellness. Racism combined with ableism creates a society where people of color living with mental health challenges are significantly disadvantaged in their chances of accessing the resources needed to aid in recovery and treatment for mental illness.

Distrust of the medical system, the lack of mental health professionals who are people of color, and the lack of financial resources for accessing mental healthcare all contribute to the growing mental health crisis. Cultural beliefs contribute to stigmatizing mental illness, especially when mental illness is thought to be caused by character flaws or result from lack of faith or personal strength. Mental illness often goes undiagnosed and untreated in communities of color.

This means millions of people every day experience the pain and suffering of mental illness, often in silence, feeling isolated and alone in their pain. This stigma and lack of access to affordable care means more than half of adults with a mental illness receive no treatment. One in five adults with mental illness are not able to get the treatment they need because of barriers. These barriers to treatment include no insurance or limited coverage, shortfall in psychiatrists and not enough mental healthcare providers, lack of available treatment types (inpatient treatment, individual therapy), disconnect between primary care systems and behavioral health systems, and lack of resources to cover out of pocket expenses, such as copayments, types of treatment not covered by their insurance, or when providers do not take their insurance.[6]

Mental Health Justice and Faith Communities

What does mental health justice look like in action? Trinity United Church of Christ in Chicago, a predominately Black congregation, is one example of how a faith community is making mental health justice and racial justice a manifestation of God's love for us. According to the church's website, they are helping create justice by providing counseling services for people in need as part of their outreach ministry. They offer quality mental health counseling by trained and licensed mental health professionals. Church members have also organized to educate one another and to advocate in various public forums for universal access to health insurance.[7]

For Trinity UCC, mental health justice is one type of justice work that is part of what it means to follow the way of Jesus. At Trinity UCC, they believe "any honest study of our Bible bears witness to Jesus' focus on the poor, the orphan, the widow, and the 'least of these'".[8] Justice is a partnership working to lift everyone up.

Starting a mental health justice ministry at the institutional level doesn't just happen, though—it begins with conversations. One of the first steps towards mental health justice is to break the silence by telling true stories and educating ourselves about mental illness. When we tell stories, mental illness gets a face and is humanized.

People with mental illness are not monsters or aliens or zombies or evil spirits. We are people like your neighbor, your co-worker, your friend, your family member, and you. When we hear the stories of others, we realize mental illness touches all of us in some way. Telling stories helps us to heal and find hope as individuals, couples, families, and communities.

We need faith leaders, theologians, preachers, chaplains, teachers, and community leaders to break the silence. We need more churches like Trinity UCC to include mental health justice as part of their ministries. We need more preachers like Trinity UCC's senior pastor, the Rev. Dr. Otis Moss III, who openly talks about his sister's death by suicide after living with schizophrenia, a severe and chronic mental illness. In "Losing Daphne," an essay published in *Ebony* magazine, Moss breaks the silence about mental illness, family, and the church. He asks the question, "How do you speak about paranoid schizophrenia to a world ignorant of mental illness?"[9]

Through sharing the personal stories of our lived experiences, we will decrease stigma and shame. The silence about mental illness prevents us from making progress towards more effective treatments to support mental health recovery. In cultures of silence, stigma, and shame, we cannot heal. Telling the truth in community is how we will begin to heal.

Mental health justice means more funding for research into prevention and treatment for mental illness. Not long ago, medical professionals were performing lobotomies, cutting out parts of the brain thought to cause mental illness. Current treatments include talk therapy, cognitive behavioral therapy (CBT) that teaches skill development and emotional regulation, brain chemistry-altering medications, and efforts to re-circuit the brain through electroconvulsive shock therapy (ECT).

Recently my brother Scott, who has lived with chronic and severe bipolar disorder for three decades, asked to have a brain transplant. It was no mere tongue-in-cheek comment—he is physically and emotionally suffering. There is still no clear solution to preventing and treating brain diseases. Much about the human brain is a mystery and remains yet to be discovered by scientific and behavioral research.

In marriage, mental health justice means treating one another with equality and respect, and yet spousal abuse of all types is not uncommon. Emotional, physical, spiritual, and sexual abuse is not part of mental health justice. Abuse causes harm and this does not fulfill God's will for our lives to flourish. When abuse is happening in a marriage or intimate relationship, no matter the cause, God wants healing and for wrongs to be righted, more than God wants the relationship to stay intact for its own sake. Sometimes justice means ending a marriage when it is no longer life-giving.

We seek the well-being of one another as part of mental health justice in our relationships. We need support systems in order to experience mental health justice in our marriages. We need accountability from others, we need care, we need other people because we are interconnected. Mental health justice happens in life-giving relationships.

Mental Illness and the Bible

The Bible is a collection of stories about God's love affair with all of Creation. It's a story about God's relationship with us and how God loves each one of us unconditionally. You might say it's a story about the ultimate blessed union. The Bible begins by telling the story of the first blessed union, uniting the spiritual world with the physical world. Written between about 1200 B.C. and the first century A.D., the Bible contains stories of human encounters with love, both earthly and divine.[10] Reading these stories and interpreting them through the lens of mental health invites us into deeper questions and insights about God's blessed union with humanity.

This ancient collection of texts includes not only stories, but also songs, poetry, love songs, letters, and history from an era long before Prozac and Zoloft. When we read the Bible today, it's important to remember the Bible was written before scientific understanding of the brain's role in influencing our behaviors, health, outlook on the world, and relationships. In the Bible, when people experienced illness, it was often thought to be for spiritual reasons.

Prior to the nineteenth century, there was no scientific language about the brain and mental illness.[11] For example, in the fourth century B.C., Aristotle considered the brain to be "a secondary organ that served as a cooling agent for the heart and a place in which spirit circulated freely".[12]

No one has ever asked me, "Did Adam and Eve experience mental illness in their blessed union, especially symptoms of PTSD and depression when they were kicked out of paradise? " But I wouldn't even blink if someone did. With new information about the human brain and mental health, we can and should ask new questions of ancient stories. If anything, asking these new questions strengthens the value of the Bible as a tool for building up our faith as we seek to better understand our connections to one another, ourselves, and to God.

If God truly loves us, then exploring the stories of God can help us experience a deepening of divine love. In lifelong engagement with the scriptures and in small group Bible studies, we experience the power of God still speaking to us. As we grow and learn and age and "life happens," we have new questions to ask and new perspectives through which we read the text.

If God is still speaking to us, what does the Bible say about mental illness? Did anyone in the Bible experience mental illness? Is God okay with us taking prescription medications as part of our treatment plan for brain disorders and diseases?

Reading the Bible with our attention focused on mental illness, we discover the prophet Elijah (1 Kings 18-19) experienced something that seems a lot like depression. Elijah won an epic battle, yet instead of feeling victorious and confident, he felt hopeless, lost, and afraid. Elijah's self-esteem was at an all-time low and he just wanted to sleep forever.

Jesus encounters people with symptoms of what today we would call mental illness (Mark 1:21-28 and Mark 5:1-20). Jesus sets an example for us in his response by showing inclusion and love to people who experience mental illness. The Bible is not silent when it comes to mental illness, nor is Jesus.

In the Bible there are more healing stories about the human troubles we now identify as mental illness than all other healing stories combined. In all of them, Jesus' response to mental illness is to engage people and show compassion. Suicide is referred to in the Bible multiple times, including the story of Jesus' disciple Judas who died by suicide (Matthew 27:3-5).

How many sermons have you preached or heard about mental illness or suicide? Most of us don't preach or hear sermons about these stories of mental illness in the Bible. Still, it would be a faithful interpretation to say that God, as revealed to us in Jesus the healer and friend, probably would have encouraged those with mental illness to follow their treatment and self-care plans, had such things existed back then. Yes, we can love Jesus and love our therapist, too. We can take our meds and meditate, too.

It is also important to talk about mental illness and sacred texts because people have spiritual questions, especially when it comes to suicide and complex health conditions. How does the God of the Bible relate to people with mental illness, yesterday and today? We wonder where God is in the midst of mental illness. We wonder if God still loves us when we have a mental illness or when loved ones die by suicide. We wonder, *does God hate me or my family? Is God punishing us with mental illness?*

Many people with mental illness have heard advice along the lines of, "you just need to have more faith" or "just pray about it more." So, what is the role of faith when it comes to mental illness? Faith may not set us free from mental illness. However, faith helps us seek after God's presence in the midst of our experiences with mental illness.

Highlighting mental illness in the Bible helps to break the silence because if the Bible talks about mental illness, then so does our still-speaking God. Our sacred texts and our faith traditions can be tools we use to break the silence about marriage and mental illness. The Good Book can be a blessing for couples looking for hope because it reminds us God promises to love us even when we "walk through the valley of the shadow" of mental illness (Psalm 23). In fact, the image of God as a caring shepherd guiding the sheep through the valley is an encouraging metaphor that God does not abandon us during difficult times. God is committed to journeying with us, especially when we need God's help the most. God will not forsake us. In the shadows of mental illness, God is with us.

Chapter Two:

Do You Promise...

I agree with those who say the decision of whom we marry is the most important personal decision we will ever make. Marriage is at its core a relationship. Marriage is a commitment. We promise to love this person with all our heart, our mind, and our soul. When our blessed union is born from love, then we can experience the mirroring of compassion in our marriage. This compassion is the blessing the marriage union brings to each individual.

Yet, we are not always compassionate toward ourselves or our partners. This is what makes marriage hard, even under the best circumstances. Given that half of marriages end in divorce, everyone who says, "I do" has a 50 percent chance of making it to the finish line—"as long as we both shall live."

Marriages need nurturing and support in order to be fulfilling and healthy. Just as we need personal wellness practices to be healthy, so do our marriages. Counseling is not only a response to a marital crisis, but marriage counseling when things are "good" helps build a stronger foundation. With guidance and support, we can learn better communication techniques, carve out space for quality time together, and discover deeper connection.

Marriages also need support from the wider community, including community conversations about how mental illness impacts our relationships. Faith communities can create forums to openly discuss the ups and downs of marriages. Spiritual support groups for couples that are impacted by mental illness can also be powerful places to find comfort, support, and healing.

Marriage and family therapists have identified several models to characterize different types of relationships married partners have with each other. In *Making Marriage Simple*, marriage theorists Harville Hendrix and Helen LaKelly Hunt introduce the model of Partnership Marriage as one approach to a healthy life together. In a Partnership Marriage the purpose of marriage is to "promote each other's psychological and spiritual growth...to experience the ultimate communion possible between humans" (pg. 4).

One of the problems with the Partnership Model, however, is that it comes from an ableist framework, assuming both partners are neuro-typical and do not live with mental illness. The Partnership Model assumes each partner is experiencing mental wellness and is equally able to carry all the household responsibilities. This model does not account for the challenging dynamics marriages face when one or both individuals experience mental health conditions. In effect, it assumes both individuals come into the marriage without severe or chronic mental illness.

Mental illness often tips the scale, throwing off balance the equality and mutuality. When a person is experiencing an episode, their ability to carry equal weight becomes compromised. Without treatment and recovery, mental illness can harm the marriage because the illness strains the sense of mutuality in the relationship. Chronic illness makes living happily ever after harder. Couples in marriages with mental illness require more support and resources to find happiness.

Another example of ableism in the Partnership Marriage model is when Hendrix and Hunt state, "married people, on average, are healthier, live longer, enjoy higher incomes, and raise healthier families...whether they are 'happy' or not" (pg. 123). The same is not true for marriages where there is mental illness and disabilities. What can we say about marriages when we know individuals with disabilities or mental health challenges on average have poorer health, live shorter lives, and make less money?

Does the "marriage advantage" apply when the marriage includes individuals with severe and/or chronic mental illness? What about the negative impact of mental illness on a marriage? We need to acknowledge that one model of marriage does not fit all, especially those that include people with mental illness and disabilities.

What if there is a "marriage disadvantage" when it comes to mental illness? Hendrix and Hunt address this, albeit without naming mental illness, saying, "We do know that stressful marriages have been shown to lower immunity and increase depression. In fact, a recent study suggests a stressful marriage can be as bad on the heart as a regular smoking habit" (pg. 128). For marriages with mental illness, there is often added stress, and stress is bad for the heart.

What I find to be true is that mental illness within a marriage negatively impacts the overall well-being of the couple and calls for additional forms of care and support in order to flourish. If you could wave a magic wand and make mental illness disappear from marriage, would you? My answer is yes. Our hearts would be happier and healthier without the stress of mental illness.

I agree that marriages with mental illness are at a disadvantage, given my personal experience and the stories I've heard from other couples. Experiencing chronic mental illness in marriage is stressful and can literally break your heart. As one friend shared about his marriage and mental illness, "I'm just tired of this being part of our life and hate the idea that it always will be." It is easy to feel overwhelmed by the possibility that things will never get better.

This is the challenge of living with chronic illness within a marriage: the emotional weight of fearing an uncertain future, which might be filled with more bad days than good. The stigma of mental illness causes us to keep these fears locked inside of us, further isolating us from resources of support. The mental illness disadvantage can make hope for a happy marriage seem out of reach.

In his memoir, *My Lovely Wife in the Psych Ward*, Mark Lukach says when he began falling in love, he didn't know his future bride lived with mental illness. Instead, he noticed his new bride's mental illness slowly emerging over time. Mark recalls how he felt in the hospital when he heard the doctor give his wife's diagnosis: schizophrenia. They both feared what the new diagnosis would mean for their marriage. She had previously experienced bouts of depression as part of bipolar disorder, and worried about living with a lifelong serious illness and he worried about being a caregiver for a person with a lifelong serious illness. It's understandable how a new diagnosis can be devastating and may seem like a life sentence.

Mental illness affects marriages in different ways. Some partners experience mental illness as the loss of the person they most love. Some people feel as though they are married to a person who is no longer the person they first fell in love with, but a shadow of their former self. I know that I am not the same person I am today as the person who said, "I do." Life changes us and experiences of mental health challenges change us. We can be changed for the better when we have the support we need for recovery, health, and wellness.

Mental illness can also change us in ways that are painful, like side effects of medications that decrease our desire for physical intimacy. It's natural for all of us to change over the course of time together, yet the change thrust upon us from mental illness is different. There is grief that comes with serious and chronic mental illness in marriage. By acknowledging the pain, we can begin to open our hearts to healing.

When we experience changes in our thoughts, feelings, moods, desires, and behaviors because of mental illness, our marriage relationship is directly impacted. After all, if marriage is a relationship and mental illness impacts how we relate to others, then perhaps our marriages, our most intimate relationship, are hit the hardest by the challenges of mental illness.

The marriage vows bind us together "in sickness and in health," and most of us understand this to include even the peculiar kind of sickness that is mental illness. Yet the struggle remains. And we are often left alone in silence wondering what we can do to make things better.

How do we love someone with a mental illness? In a NAMI blog post titled "How To Love Someone With A Mental Illness," the writer notes, "Choosing to love someone who acts or feels unlovable can be part of what helps them see they are valued as a whole person, they are not the sum total of their pain...Mental illnesses are *illnesses*, and sometimes they can change someone's circumstances...they can even change their personalities for a time, change their interests, their spirit. **But they are the same person you have always loved**, and they need you to see that person in them—even when they can't see themselves clearly"[13] (emphasis mine).

After all, mental illness does not change the fact we are beloved children of God. Even though they are the same person you have always loved, it can be hard to recognize them. Looking through God's eyes helps us to see past the label and the diagnosis.

A great example of "choosing to love" came to me through a story from my friend Monique. Over lunch, I asked Monique what I thought was a philosophical question about marriage and mental illness. The conversation turned personal very quickly, however.

Monique shared with me that her vision for her marriage is to flourish, knowing both she and her partner have mental illness. She said flourishing for their marriage happens when they are up front with each other about their mental health status, can state their needs, and can get the support they need.

I listened in awe as Monique described how her marriage has a wellness plan in place for any time one partner becomes sick. I knew about wellness plans for individuals, but to have one for a marriage was a new concept for me. She said the plan simply goes into effect when the need arises, with no pressure for the sick partner to "snap out of it." The person is allowed to be sick. Given the permission to be sick, they can then work on getting healthier without shame, judgment, or stigma. This plan is brilliant and seems to be working well for their marriage.

During these times, the couple rely on therapists, close friends, and circles of additional support. They realize that it is unfair to expect each other to fulfill all of each other's emotional needs. Monique and her partner figured out a way to remove the frustration, burden, and disappointment by taking this unrealistic expectation off the altar.

What if the church talked more about marriage wellness plans and how people can flourish in marriages with mental illness? This type of conversation about a mental health wellness plan needs to be part of every premarital counseling program. We can take steps now to help couples prepare for a future where they are likely to experience some form of mental illness, whether mild or severe, in their marriage.

One thing is for sure: mental illness makes marriage more complex. As such, it has pushed me to think about alternative models for this unique relationship. The Partnership Model isn't a good fit for marriages with mental health challenges. But, as with everything else, before we can look at creating a new model for marriage, we need to first have the conversations and break the silence. I hope the stories in this book will inspire others to create alternative models of marriage that are informed by disabilities and mental health justice.

So, let's just talk for a while about mental illness and marriage. Rodney, a friend who is married and lives with mental illness, told me about the exhaustion he felt with the ongoing work required to navigate life with his partner. Rodney said, "I'm not getting anywhere. Even though things are better on the whole, I'm feeling so worn down." He told me he felt tired of being sick.

Rodney confessed to feeling guilty for having a mental illness. Guilt about something we don't have a lot of control over is especially burdensome. He said trying to talk to his wife was like repeating the same conversation over and over again. While not overtly rejecting his pain, it's clear she expects him to somehow "power through" the days. He said, "I'm just sad. And hurt."

Rodney realized that each time he experienced a disruptive episode of mental illness, he felt more disconnected from his wife. He worried about his marriage ending because of mental illness. Will it always be this way? It takes courage and faith to be vulnerable and authentic when breaking the silence. The good news is we give each other power by telling true stories. So, I'll follow Rodney's example and share one of my own.

My Marriage and Mental Illness

I've been married to my husband for fifteen years. I learned early on in my marriage that even though people make jokes about the problems married couples have...he said, she said... toilet seat up or down...nobody was really talking about how our own mental health and our partner's mental health impact the marriage relationship. I found myself feeling alone when I began to struggle to take care of my own mental health, while also supporting my partner in his mental health. I felt especially alone when I noticed what was happening to our blessed union.

Early on in my marriage, I felt regretful, scared. I blamed myself for our frequent unhappiness. I thought, "What have I done? What will we do? How can we save our marriage from mental illness?"

One day, after years of individual therapy, I realized I had married a person whose quirks and personality combined various elements of my family of origin. It was no surprise I chose to marry a person living with mental illness—after all, love shaped by mental illness was familiar to me from my own family upbringing. This phenomenon is known as Imago theory (*Getting the Love You Want: A Guide for Couples*, Third Edition. Hendrix and Hunt, 2007). According to this theory, I unconsciously married someone who manifests symptoms of mental illness because they reflect the behaviors of the people who most directly shaped my childhood experiences of love.

My first book, *Blessed Are the Crazy: Breaking the Silence About Mental Illness, Family and Church,* tells my stories of growing up with a father who died from untreated mental illness, and a brother who is on full disability for bipolar disorder. It also describes witnessing my cousin's execution for committing a murder while in a psychotic episode. According to Imago theory, I've got to work through my adverse childhood experiences and childhood wounds caused by mental illness in order to get the love I want.

Nobody wakes up one morning and says, "Someday I want to marry a person with a chronic brain disease." But as someone whose marriage is affected by chronic mental illness, I believe it is possible to live together in a blessed union. It is not easy, but it is possible.

Since mental illness is invisible, we may not even realize our partner has mental illness or that we do as well. We could go for years with untreated mental illness and never know it. Breaking the silence about mental illness and marriage allows us to prepare ourselves for the realities of the road ahead and get the support we need from our faith community and mental health professionals.

Looking back, during our premarital counseling sessions, of which there were several, not once did the topic of physical or mental health arise. The premarital counselor didn't talk about sex or mental illness and neither did we. Perhaps we could have brought up the topic, but honestly, I was afraid to.

I wanted to start a *new* life and a *new* family, not bring my *old* life and *old* family along with me. When we said our marriage vows before God, one another, our family, and friends, we had no idea about the mental illness we had married into, the multiple mental illnesses passed down through the generations from both sides of the family.

We did not know about the addiction, anxiety, depression, and bipolar disorder that silently ran in our families' bloodstreams. We did not talk about the stories of our divorced parents and the adverse experiences peppering our childhoods. Those were the stories we chose not to tell each other during our sushi dinners or late-night walks. We did our own unconscious, careful curating of the narratives of our lives, leaving out anything unflattering or unsexy.

It's not that we intentionally hid these truths from each other. I imagine they were truths so deeply buried inside of us, they were not even developed as conscious thoughts at the time. Shame and stigma buried our truths.

Looking back, I realize now in the course of our three years of dating and engagement, I did not tell my partner the whole truth about my father's bipolar disorder. He did not tell me the whole truth about his father's alcoholism. Sharing those facts seemed then as absurd as it would be now to advertise on an online dating portfolio: "daughter of delusional, mentally ill homeless man seeks son of a drunk."

It wasn't until our wedding day that the groom met the father of the bride. My husband remembers the first and last thing my dad said to him. It was a conspiracy theory involving the Queen of England. My dad died from mental illness-related causes six months later. Our wedding day was the last day we saw my father alive. The last thing my father said to me was that he was proud of me and that he loved me. It was the most coherent my father had been in years.

On October 14, 2006, when my husband and I were joined together in holy marriage, I did not know the extent of his depression, addiction, and anxiety, and he did not know the nature of my posttraumatic stress disorder. Neither of us really knew these facts about ourselves. Three years later we would bring a child into this great unknown and learn to navigate marriage and family life with mental illness. Marriage and parenthood with mental illness adds more complexity and more challenges. More stress to the heart, that's for sure.

Over a decade later, I'd like to say our home is the warm blazing hearth where a community gathers, but the truth is, it's not. At the best of times we manage to stay covered in the warm blankets of therapy (individual, marriage, and family) and, in so doing, succeed at keeping the chill of the illnesses at bay. At the worst of times, we look for the escape route, often finding a dead end. These bad days motivate us to do our individual and collective work of recovery because we know life can get better.

Yes, despite our best efforts through wellness practices such as exercise, healthy eating, getting enough sleep combined with therapy and medication, mental illness still has a way of sneaking into our marriage and family life. It starts with a dulling. A glazed over look. An expressionless face. Eyes no longer sparkling. Arms no longer embracing. Bodies no longer touching. Shoulders slouching and a head looking down. When I first see these physical signs of depression, it is a warning to me that today is not going to be a good day as a family.

Today daddy needs a break. It's a day for mommy and kid time. Today is a day for going to the library, and going to the grocery store, and going to the beach, and driving in the car. Today is a day for daddy to be alone.

My body knew this pattern before my mind knew, and my heart was the last to know. I would see the signs in my partner, and reflexively hold my son closer and tighter. I would move quicker around the house. I would speak less and plan more. What slowly emerged out of this first year as new parents was the unsettling feeling that there was something seriously wrong.

My partner's lack of interest, lack of pleasure, lack of ability to engage continued over several weeks. I can relate to author Mark Lukach who in an interview with PBS said about his partner, "I lived and breathed alongside [her] depression, studying it for patterns and clues for what was working and what wasn't. It wasn't my diagnosis, but it consumed my life".[14]

We got to a point where my partner realized he needed to get help for his mental health. Thankfully, he wanted the help. And ever since then he has been actively engaged in his recovery and mental wellness. We feel very lucky and privileged. We have health insurance, access to quality mental healthcare, and the resources such as time and flexible work schedules that support the work of ongoing recovery for both of us.

Even with all the supports in place, even when you do "all of the right things," there are still bad days, bad weeks, and bad months. In the summer of 2019, I discovered during a marriage counseling session that my partner was living with thoughts of suicide. I had no idea that his depression had gotten so bad. I was shocked, scared, and worried. We turned to our support system to help us. Thankfully, a combination of individual therapy, marriage counseling, a new psychiatrist, new medication, and a NAMI support group helped us get through this difficult time. Coming out of this suicidal episode, realizing I could have lost him forever, I felt a deeper sense of urgency to work on our health and wholeness, both in our marriage and as individuals.

For our marriage, we have found the model of Partnership Marriage to be helpful. Because it doesn't consider mental illness, we supplemented and adapted the approach. In addition to marriage therapy, we also are both in individual therapy to help address the dynamics of our own mental health challenges and how they impact our marriage. For example, I survived emotional and verbal abuse as well as neglect by my father in childhood. A deep emotional wound I bring into our marriage is fear of angry verbal outbursts.

When my husband expresses anger, in what for most partners would seem an appropriate way, I am triggered and become a helpless child inside who wants to flee the scene—or the entire relationship. I am hypersensitive to yelling and any body language expressing anger. Individual therapy helps me to realize these dynamics, to understand them, and to name them.

In therapy, I honor myself and honor the fact that I am on a healing journey, and healing takes time. It turns out, individual therapy is also good for my marriage. I cannot just point my finger to my husband and blame him for our marital challenges. It's me, too.

In Partnership Marriage, one of the core tenets is the belief we are all wounded in relationship and the only way we can heal is in relationship. Marriage becomes the key relationship that heals us when "we each answer the call to become each other's healers" (*Making Marriage Simple*, pg. 56). Can a marriage with mental illness still be a healing relationship where we both become "each other's healers"? Can a person with mental illness be a healer?

So far in my own marriage, the answer is "Yes, but." Yes...but it is more complicated and takes more work. If "healing happens only in a safe environment" (*Making Marriage Simple*, pg. 53) then it takes more work for me to feel like I am safe. This is the hard work I do in individual therapy and this is the hard work my husband does in his therapy.

We each have our own recovery work to do as individuals. He works on his anger management, and I work on embodying my power and authority. He has learned that when he is feeling angry around me, it is best to remove himself from the situation. Later, after the emotion has passed, he can talk through problems with me and we can resolve them. I've learned to trust anger to teach me something and I do not have to be afraid.

When I am feeling frightened, I breathe deeply and mentally ground myself in my body, bringing my awareness to the present moment. The practice of restorative yoga also helps me to breathe through any emotional or physical discomfort I may feel and to remember this fear is temporary. It will pass. I continue to pray.

I am deeply encouraged in my marriage by knowing both of us are committed to work for our own well-being and to support the well-being of each other. This mutual commitment is key for our marriage's survival and thriving. I also know that my physical health is tied to my emotional health, and this is all tied to the health of our marriage. In this way, we embody our marriages. Our bodies continue to be on a healing journey as we recover in mind, body, and spirit from the traumas of our past. Our love is physical, not only in the intimate expressions of lovemaking, but also in how our bodies carry and express our emotions.

Gary Chapman, in his best-selling book *The Five Love Languages*, says, "When your spouse's emotional love tank is full and he feels secure in your love, the whole world looks bright and your spouse will move out to reach his highest potential in life. But when the love tank is empty and he feels used but not loved, the whole world looks dark and he will likely never reach his potential for good in the world." (page 37)

What happens when we read Chapman's words through the lens of mental illness? What happens when mental illness causes the love in the tank to evaporate, in spite of a partner's best efforts to keep it full? What happens when mental illness and the side effects of psychiatric medications cause the sex drive to dry up?

As I read Chapman's words about an empty love tank, I am reminded of my husband during a depressive episode. It's an eerily perfect description of how I observe him feeling: used but not loved, with the whole world looking dark, like he will never reach his potential for good in the world. One of the most tragic dynamics of mental illness in marriage is how it empties our tank of feelings of love and the desire to make love. The heart and the body need love in order to keep going. Marriages need love in order to thrive.

Chapman also notes that "the emotional need for love must be met if we are to have emotional health. Married adults long to feel affection and love from their spouses. We feel secure when we are assured that our mate accepts us, wants us, and is committed to our well-being" (*The Five Love Languages*, pg. 33). Here again, mental illness sucks away our ability to feel accepted, wanted, and the object of our partner's desire and commitment. Mental illness makes us feel the opposite: we feel insecure, rejected, unaccepted, unwanted, ugly, and alone. How do we create a blessed union when we feel this way? Where is there hope for a better future? Where is the bonding that happens when we feel loved and make love?

We find hope for a better future in our blessed union through our mutual, unwavering commitment to individual and collective mental and physical wellness. Every day we are working towards healing, both as individuals and as a couple at the same time. Hendrix and Hunt say,

> Committing to share a life with someone else is an honor and a responsibility. And we don't use those words lightly. The role of those choosing to commit to a life partner is that of friend, supporter, advocate, and healer. It is about growing oneself to take on the welfare of the other. It is about committing to create a healthy relationship, in order to mature as an individual. (*Making Marriage Simple*, pg. 140).

Thinking of ourselves not only as husband and wife, but also as advocate and healer feels like a more honest reflection of our marriage. We are advocates and healers for ourselves and for one another—mind, body, and spirit.

We need to balance being an advocate for ourselves as well as an advocate for our partner. Being both a healer of ourselves as well as a healer for our partner. Being a friend to ourselves as well as a friend to our partner. If we only focus on ourselves, we are not loving our partner. If we only focus on our partner, we are not loving ourselves. Balancing the giving and the receiving of love honors the covenant of marriage.

To share a life together is to share this journey of healing. This is the truth my marriage has taught me: we need one another to heal. We need one another to experience mental wellness for our hearts to be healthy.

In my own marriage, my partner and I have come to appreciate how much we have changed, healed, and grown as individuals since we stood at the church altar. We have had illnesses and job loss, moved across country, traveled around the world, and become parents. It helps us heal to understand how mental illness impacts our experiences of life in ways that are different from marriages without mental illness.

Honestly, there were times when divorce seemed to be the best option, yet even then, we sensed our problems were fixable and things could get better with focused effort and hard work. While there were moments of hopelessness about the future of our marriage, sadness about how far apart we felt from one another, these feelings of despair didn't last forever. There is a lesson to be found here. For our blessed union we discovered that if we walked through the shadows in the valley of mental illness long enough, the light of healing began to emerge on the other side of the valley.

For us, we knew our marriage could be better. We knew it would take both of us working hard to improve it. We set about the work of healing ourselves and each other, one day at a time. We embraced this new calling as individuals and as a couple. With purpose and intention, we decided this work of healing— mentally and physically—was a top priority for our marriage.

Realizing that our marriage itself had symptoms of mental illness gave us insight into how to change our relationship and make it healthier. Couples who learn how mental illness affects their marriages often experience a breakthrough when they view mental illness as not only a diagnosis for one of them, but a diagnosis for the marriage. Marriages with mental illness can recover, too.

Mark Lukach, in the interview quoted earlier, said of his partner's bipolar disorder diagnosis, "We chose to redefine her illness as something we shared: ours, and not just hers. Not one voice over the other, but both voices, with equal weight and validity, even when in disagreement. Bipolar disorder had been tearing us apart. But this subtle change of a pronoun from 'hers' to 'ours' transformed it into something that could bring us together".[15] This view upholds justice in the marriage. Both partners are treated with respect and the burden of mental illness is shared equally.

The struggle is real yet so many of us—millions—are suffering in silence. The truth is marriages are in a mental health crisis. I believe the church can be a place for these honest conversations to begin.

Not everyone wants to open up in a religious setting, though. Couples are afraid of being judged. They are afraid of getting hurt. They are afraid of being rejected and deemed damaged and unlovable. How can we allow these fears to fester in the church? What might we do instead?

Beginning in 2018, as part of my work serving the United Church of Christ on the national staff as the Minister for Disabilities and Mental Health Justice, I have had the privilege to speak with church leaders and church members from diverse backgrounds on the topics of disabilities and mental health justice. In this role, I am invited to participate in the national conversation about faith and mental health. On one of the national committees for mental health where I served in a leadership role, I met Kay Warren, who cofounded Saddleback Church with her husband Rick Warren.

In a blog post, Kay shared about the time when her husband Rick, a high-profile mega church senior pastor "got physically sick from depression and was hospitalized because he couldn't function; he was fainting. I remember sobbing constantly, thinking: 'This is not the way I thought life was going to be; this is not the way I thought marriage was going to be.' We just kept thinking it was our fault—that we were bad Christians...".[16]

Kay learned what many other faith leaders also affirm: people with mental illness are not bad people, and Christians with mental illness are not bad Christians. We can no longer blame God, our faith, or our marriages for mental illness. It's time to have this conversation about marriage and mental illness in a way that honors the institution of marriage and the complex realities of mental health conditions. It's time to ask the hard questions about what happens when mental illness tests the limits of our love.

Over the years I have paid close attention to others' stories about mental illness and marriage. It seems like most marriages have a story about how one or both partners' mental health condition impacted them. There is no shame in experiencing mental illness because it is a common part of human life. We need to free ourselves from shame.

The more open and honest we can be about our lives, the better our chances are for flourishing. Mental health thrives in the light and mental illness grows in the shadows. Together we are shining a light on mental illness and marriage.

Through the telling of true stories, we are healing. I am grateful for all who have trusted me with their stories and given me their permission to share them with you. Hold these stories close to your heart. Hold these couples in your prayers.

Hold onto the truth: you are God's beloved. Hold onto your own blessed union with God, the divine relationship which is the foundation for all human love. Hold onto hope.

God's Love and Mental Illness

According to the Book of Worship of the United Church of Christ (the Christian denomination I serve), "The essence of marriage is a covenanted commitment that has its foundation in the faithfulness of God's love." A covenant is a promise made in earnest, a promise to keep. We make promises because God is a promise-maker. It is God's promise to love us, creating the foundation for the covenant of marriage.

The Bible shows us the love of God as recorded through human history, from the birth of the universe in Genesis to the birth of the way of Jesus in the Gospels and ending in Revelation with a vision for a future realm where love reigns supreme. As the Hebrew prophets proclaimed, love keeps God in relationship with us and love keeps us in relationship with God. God's love knits us together in our mother's womb (Psalm 139:19). The apostle Paul says God's love holds us together as the Body of Christ (1 Cor. 12).

If God is love (1 John 4:8), then God does not punish us with diseases, disorders, and mental illness. God's love is what helps us to walk through the shadow of mental illness. God's love endures mental illness. God's love is where hope is planted. In God we experience the fullness of life's blessings no matter who we are or where we are on life's journey. God loves us in mental illness and in mental health.

If the foundation of the marriage covenant is the faithfulness of God's love, then how does God's love show up in marriages where the relationship is affected by mental illness? What happens to a marriage where one or both partners experiences mental illness?

How do we keep our promises when mental illness tries to break them apart? How do you love someone with mental illness? How do you feel loved while at the same time feelings of worthlessness and self-loathing threaten to take over?

To begin answering those questions, let's look for a minute at the marriage vows many of us have taken. Then let's read through a Bible passage often read at weddings: 1 Corinthians 13. Over the next seven chapters, we will hear some true stories about marriage and mental illness. I have changed names and some identifying details about the couples to protect their privacy, and sometimes combined pieces of more than one story to create a composite. We will reflect on questions like those listed above. And we will explore what it might mean to love, to comfort, to honor, to bear with, to be faithful, and to love as long as we both shall live in mental illness and in marriage.

My friend Tony shared with me about his marriage and mental illness: "There are so many frustrating things about it—how simple responsibilities become overwhelming, how that means more on my plate, how her mood affects mine, how it can deflate whatever joy you might feel in an instant. I pray that this gets better soon and that I can summon some patience and grace." Tony found support for his marriage by having a safe place to share his struggles and to ask for prayer. Sometimes breaking the silence in a safe place is the first step towards hope.

Praying helps. While prayer does not cure us from mental illness, prayer brings us comfort. I pray every day for my husband's mental health. Praying for my husband is something I can do to show my support for him. He tells me that my prayers for him help.

The stories that follow and your reflections on them are a prayer...for the God of Love to give us all daily patience, grace, and hope for the journey through the valley of the shadow of mental illness.

The Marriage Vows

Will you have this one to be your beloved,
  to live together in holy marriage?
Will you love them, comfort them, honor and keep them,
  in sickness and in health,
and forsaking all others, be faithful to them
  as long as you both shall live?

The Love Passage

1 Corinthians 13

If I speak in the tongues of mortals and of angels, but do not have love, I am a noisy gong or a clanging cymbal. And if I have prophetic powers, and understand all mysteries and all knowledge, and if I have all faith, so as to remove mountains, but do not have love, I am nothing. If I give away all my possessions, and if I hand over my body so that I may boast, but do not have love, I gain nothing.

Love is patient; love is kind; love is not envious or boastful or arrogant or rude. It does not insist on its own way; it is not irritable or resentful; it does not rejoice in wrongdoing, but rejoices in the truth. It bears all things, believes all things, hopes all things, endures all things.

Love never ends. But as for prophecies, they will come to an end; as for tongues, they will cease; as for knowledge, it will come to an end. For we know only in part, and we prophesy only in part; but when the complete comes, the partial will come to an end. When I was a child, I spoke like a child, I thought like a child, I reasoned like a child; when I became an adult, I put an end to childish ways. For now we see in a mirror, dimly, but then we will see face to face. Now I know only in part; then I will know fully, even as I have been fully known. And now faith, hope, and love abide, these three; and the greatest of these is love.

Chapter Three:

To Love

If I speak in the tongues of mortals and of angels, but do not have love,
I am a noisy gong or a clanging cymbal. And if I have prophetic powers,
and understand all mysteries and all knowledge, and if I have all faith,
so as to remove mountains, but do not have love, I am nothing.
(1 Corinthians 13:1-2)

In my marriage, sometimes the noisy gongs and clanging cymbals of our arguing about whose view of reality is correct can drown out the love we want to communicate to each other. It's hard to say you are enjoying quality time with your partner when there's nothing but noise. Mental illness is a noisy gong. This invitation from scripture to see love as our ultimate possession, the thing above all others to have, reminds me to quiet my mind and refocus my thoughts.

Love is not an argument. Love is not a battle to be won. Love is not a prison. Love is the opposite of nothing. Love is everything.

Gary Chapman, author of *The Five Love Languages*, says, "The need to feel loved by one's spouse is at the heart of marital desires...Something in our nature cries out to be loved by another. Isolation is devastating to the human psyche. That is why solitary confinement is considered the cruelest form of punishments. At the heart of humankind's existence is the desire to be intimate and to be loved by another. Marriage is designed to meet that need for intimacy and love" (pg. 22).

I want to introduce you to Tom and Yoko. In this story of mental illness and marriage, we are going to hear about how Tom and Yoko experience love as something that holds them together and pushes them apart throughout their marriage as they both experience the challenges of mental illness. Tom and Yoko came to realize having love includes having enough love for themselves as individuals first.

The Blessed Union of Tom and Yoko

When I interviewed them, Tom and Yoko had celebrated five years of marriage. Tom and Yoko first connected online through a dating website and they both work in the technology industry. Tom is Jewish and Yoko is Christian. They shared this information, plus a little about their cultural background, on their dating profiles: Tom's family were third generation Russian immigrants and Yoko's family were first generation Japanese immigrants.

What Tom and Yoko didn't include on their dating profiles was the fact that they each grew up with adverse childhood experiences (ACE), including physical, emotional, and verbal abuse, and neglect. The more ACEs a person encounters early on in life, the higher likelihood of developing mental illness later in life.

Over time Tom and Yoko found out that even though they have different cultural backgrounds, they both came from families that experienced poverty, divorce, and emotional instability. Yoko's mother divorced her father when Yoko was three, fleeing an abusive husband. Yoko noticed that her mother never complained about the challenges of being a single parent, but instead worked nonstop in order to support Yoko and her little brother.

Tom's parents divorced when Tom was seven. He was the youngest of five children and he split his time between his mother and father. With his mother's second marriage came three stepsiblings. Tom was constantly bullied by his older stepbrothers and when he was old enough to tell the judge, he requested to live with his father fulltime. Even though Tom's father was an alcoholic, drinking himself to sleep every night, at least he was kind to him. It was better than the abuse Tom experienced with his stepfamily.

Even though mental illness was part of both Tom and Yoko's childhoods, mental health was not something that either Tom or Yoko heard talked about in their families growing up. What connected them most deeply was their optimism and the ability to find the good in the midst of the bad, to find pleasure in the simple things in life.

Neither Tom nor Yoko consider themselves very religious, even though early on in their marriage they attended the Catholic church on holidays like Christmas Eve and Easter because they enjoyed the special music and they liked the priest's homilies. Tom appreciated the ways Judaism and Christianity both taught the guiding principle: love your neighbor as yourself. Their favorite thing to do together when they took a day for themselves was to visit new exhibits in the museums, eat lunch in the café, and then walk outside in the gardens.

Tom's mental illness began as a teenager in his senior year of high school. He used substances to self-medicate for his anxiety, and lived with several addictions, including alcohol he sneaked from his father and opioids he got at school. He started to experience delusions and felt invincible. At the time, his behaviors flew under the radar of the adults around him (his father and teachers). He spent much of his teen years alone. He was clinically depressed, and nobody seemed to notice.

Yoko was sexually assaulted in her freshman year of college, which led to posttraumatic stress disorder (PTSD). She pushed down feelings of helplessness and shame, trying to focus on keeping her academic scholarship. Her PTSD caused her to feel powerless and afraid of situations outside of her control. She often felt anxious and had a hard time falling asleep at night, no matter how tired she felt. She didn't want to talk about what happened and coped by drinking alcohol to numb her pain. She kept her scholarships, which she was proud of, but this sense of pride faded quickly whenever she had a flashback of her sexual assault. Later in her marriage to Tom, she began experiencing depression. She was angry at herself for being depressed. She thought depression only happened to people who were mentally weak.

Tom and Yoko met the summer after college graduation. They fell in love while under the influence of drugs and alcohol, which masked their mental illnesses. The experience of falling in love itself mimicked mental illness, with its own episodes of highs and lows. In the beginning of their marriage life was good in the sense that they truly enjoyed one another's company. Despite their mental illnesses, they both felt safe with each other and loved for the first time.

During their fifth year of marriage, the twins were born. Although they were elated to have children after several years of infertility treatments, the demands of caring for twins, along with a combination of stress and lack of sleep, triggered Tom's first severe panic attack. It turned into a medical emergency. The couple, along with their three-week-old newborns, went to the emergency room. Tom was tested for signs of heart attack. The twins both picked up a virus, and came down with a 104-degree fever later that day, which added to the stress the family experienced.

When they came home, having been reassured Tom's heart was all right, Yoko urged Tom to go see a doctor about this life-altering experience of anxiety. After talking with his doctor, Tom learned his anxiety and depression could be treated through daily medications, exercise, and healthy sleep habits. It turned out Tom's illness was not related to heart disease, but to a brain disease, and the health of his whole body was connected. Over the years, Tom continued to check in with his doctor about his meds and kept up with the healthy behaviors as part of his treatment plan.

They would soon realize it was not only Tom who needed outside support. Yoko was exhausted. Breastfeeding, changing diapers, and keeping the twins alive demanded all her energy and time in those first few months. She also found herself feeling anxious and nervous about the twins' development. She lost her desire to do the things she used to enjoy, like going to movies or to church or riding her bike. From attending moms' groups, Yoko learned other new moms also felt this way. Yet, she wondered, "is this normal?"

As the first months of parenting twins went by, the lack of sleep began to negatively impact Tom and Yoko's marriage. Neither was interested in sex anymore as the twins seemed to be a constant presence and captivated Yoko's every waking hour. Yoko continued to experience PTSD from her sexual assault years before. It made her feel like she was floating above her own body during sex, as if she were another person looking down onto their bed. Yoko felt like a bad wife.

As the twins grew, and Yoko went back to work, Tom picked up more of the parenting responsibilities but often felt lonely, depressed, and overwhelmed. On Tom's good days, he enjoyed playing with the twins and nurturing their imagination with games. On his bad days, his frustration would overwhelm him, and his anxiety and depression expressed themselves in outbursts of rage. This scared the twins and Yoko. But they didn't know who they could tell or what they could do about it. Tom's earlier anxiety had played out as a possible heart problem, which had led them to seek medical care—but the anger was different somehow.

Yoko thought about calling the priest at the Catholic church but felt too ashamed to talk to him. As much as she wanted someone to soothe her fears, she didn't want to expose Tom to criticism for his anger. And mainly, she was ashamed about feeling regretful—about her babies, her husband, and her life. She couldn't bring herself to face the judgment and whispers she imagined would come from people at church noticing her imperfections and flaws. Her life wasn't perfect, and she knew it.

Also, the twins were not yet baptized, and this gnawed at her. Yoko didn't know if Tom wanted to raise their children in the Christian faith. What if Tom wanted them raised in the Jewish faith? She felt stupid for never discussing it before they were born and now she was afraid to bring it up.

Without going to church for so long, Yoko wondered whether God even cared about her. God seemed so far away. She didn't feel like she mattered to God. Did God love her? She didn't know. She felt she had disappointed God and wasted the life God gave her.

One day when the twins were a year old, Yoko left them at home with Tom while she traveled out of town for a work trip. She called Tom to check on him and the twins. Tom admitted to Yoko he was having a rough time.

Yoko could hear the twins screaming in the background. She asked Tom what happened, and he said he just "couldn't f--- ing do this anymore." Yoko's heart dropped into the pit of her stomach.

Yoko remembered her own mother's pattern of nonstop work. There were times when her mother would even disappear "for work." She would be gone for days at a time, not bothering to call home. Even when she was present, she withheld love and affection, serving up anger and resentment instead to Yoko and her brother. It was emotional abuse. Living with this trauma from childhood, Yoko was hyperalert to experiences of neglect in the home. When signs of emotional disturbance began to appear in her own nuclear family, Yoko panicked. Hearing the twins scream and her husband's emotional outburst of frustration on the phone, while she was miles away, triggered her fears—her heart raced, her thoughts went to worst-case scenario catastrophes, and she wanted to run home.

Thinking quickly, as soon as she got off the phone with Tom, she called her neighbors and asked if they could check on Tom and the twins that night. Thankfully, the neighbors brought over some brownies and visited for a while. Then they called Yoko to reassure her that her husband and the twins were going to be okay.

The neighbors offered to come over and babysit the next day so Tom could get out of the house. Yoko appreciated the support and knew that she would need to find more of it if their marriage was going to survive. She wondered if there was anyone at church she could turn to, yet shame kept her from reaching out to her church community for help.

Assured the twins would be all right, Yoko tried to get some sleep. Yet her thoughts turned to uncertainty about the marriage. She worried that she had made a horrible decision in marrying Tom. She never imagined, standing at the altar at church on her wedding day, that her life with Tom would turn into an emotional rollercoaster.

Yoko wondered if there were signs she missed when they were dating. She blamed herself for not noticing Tom's mental illness. Would she still have married him if she knew then what she knew now? What led her to marry someone with mental illness?

When Yoko got back from her work trip, she talked to Tom about them both needing professional mental health support. They sought out marriage counseling and signed up for bi-weekly appointments. They realized if their blessed union was going to survive mental illness, building a healthy marriage and family life needed to take priority.

The gift Tom and Yoko give to each other today is their time, energy, and attention to honoring their marriage vows. The relationship is not one sided; both husband and wife are all in. They also realized that alcohol was covering up and silencing big emotions that needed to be seen and heard. Tom's doctor referred him to an outpatient treatment center for addictions. Yoko found talk therapy and swimming helped her recover from the PTSD and keeps her depression at bay.

Living a sober life without the use of alcohol, Tom and Yoko began to explore other ways of relaxing, like playing board games and going for walks. They find with improved mental health, they also had more interest in physical intimacy and sex. Working on their treatment and recovery as individuals and as a couple, Tom and Yoko are learning each day about sober joy and how to love each other without using alcohol.

Given all Tom and Yoko have experienced, they felt a calling to be part of the movement to break the silence about mental illness and marriage. Yoko got up the courage to ask Tom about baptizing the children and he agreed, as long as he could still teach them about Judaism. They set up an appointment to talk to their priest about baptizing the twins. The priest was open hearted and willing to work with the family after hearing about the struggles they were experiencing.

After the baptism, they started attending worship services more often. They discovered attending church more regularly helped them focus on creating more healthy habits—socially, physically, and mentally.

As part of Tom and Yoko's healing journey toward feeling less alone and isolated, and to continue strengthening their marriage, they made a commitment to widen their circle of support. They knew that they were not alone in their struggles with mental illness and marriage. Tom and Yoko didn't want other couples to experience the same isolation and shame they had felt. They were eager to hear other couples' stories about marriage and mental illness. They asked the priest if they could start a marriage support group at the church. The priest supported this idea and helped them launch this new ministry.

Tom and Yoko realized God's love could still be found in their relationship, especially when they asked for help. When they got the support they needed, their love for each other deepened. They realized mental illness could be treated and they could find happiness in their marriage. It was a blessed union after all.

Mental Illnesses: Addiction, Anxiety, Depression, Posttraumatic Stress Disorder

Addiction is a chronic brain disease that causes you to use substances compulsively despite their harmful consequences. Many people experience both addiction and another mental illness. Sometimes people use substances to self-medicate their mental illness. Stopping the use of substances is one part of the recovery process. Another part of recovery is treating the whole person, including their medical, psychological, social, and spiritual needs.

Anxiety is a reaction to fear or stress. Anxiety is a normal part of everyday life, such as worrying about taking a test. Anxiety becomes a health condition when it is excessive, involves unfounded dread of everyday situations and interferes with your life. Anxiety disorder is one of the most common mental illnesses and takes many forms: panic disorder, obsessive-compulsive disorder, social anxiety disorder, agoraphobia, a specific phobia, and generalized anxiety disorder.

Depression is a medical condition affecting how you feel, think, and act. The primary sign of major depression is an extended time of at least two weeks of feeling sad and having no interest or pleasure in normal activities (such as eating, socializing, sex, and recreation). Depression is more intense and longer in duration than sadness. Depression drains energy and pleasure from you and can manifest in physical pain such as body aches or headaches as well as mood and emotional symptoms. Other common symptoms include changes in appetite, sleep changes, agitation, feelings of worthlessness or guilt, problems thinking and concentrating and making decisions, fatigue, and thoughts of death or suicide. Depression can take many forms: major depressive disorder, persistent depressive disorder, and postpartum depression.

Posttraumatic Stress Disorder (PTSD) is what can occur after you experience or witness a situation involving harm or the threat of harm. PTSD symptoms include being startled easily, being unable to feel positive emotions, experiencing flashbacks, or being quick to upset. People with PTSD can be triggered by images, sounds, smells, and events that recall past trauma.

Love and Mental Illness

Love is the Bible's main message. In the Bible, love exists in our three primary relationships: with God, self, and other. The Bible says we love because God first loved us (1 John 4:19). God is the creator of love and we are created to love in relationship. Our love for God, for our partner, and for ourselves can be tested and challenged by mental illness.

Tom and Yoko both made a promise on their wedding day to love someone who lives with mental illness even if they did not realize it at the time. Mental illness was a big surprise. Standing at the altar before God, family, and friends, neither one consciously said, "I promise to love you in mental illness and in health." But their vow to love each other remains. For couples like Tom and Yoko, love cannot be defined or limited by their mental illness. Love is more powerful than mental illness.

Depression impacts our faith in complex ways. It's hard to believe in God when everything hurts. It's hard to have faith in God when we don't feel supported by our faith community. It's hard to feel God's love for us when our mental illness empties our love tank. Instead of being victims of mental illness, Tom and Yoko took steps to break the silence about mental illness and marriage. In so doing, they discovered they were still loved and blessed by God. In starting the support group for couples at their church, they transformed their experiences of suffering into a life-giving ministry.

The apostle Paul wrote 1 Corinthians 13 for a faith community experiencing division and conflict. Life was hard. Like a distressed couple, this expression of the early church was thinking about divorcing.[17] Paul wanted to help. Though we often hear this passage included in wedding ceremonies as a way to celebrate human romantic love, its purpose is to remind us of our ultimate source of love: God.

When things get tough in any relationship, whether that's in church or in our marriages, we need encouragement to choose the more excellent way (1 Corinthians 12:31). We need God's help to sustain us in the struggle to love and to stay united in our blessed union as we seek to overcome great challenges and hardship. Seeking our Higher Power as our source for unconditional love provides an endless supply from which to draw in difficult times.

The message in the Bible is that nothing can separate us from the love of God. In his letter to the church in Rome, the apostle Paul writes, "For I am sure that neither death nor life, nor angels nor rulers, nor things present nor things to come, nor powers, nor height nor depth, nor anything else in all creation, will be able to separate us from the love of God in Christ Jesus our Lord" (Romans 8: 38-39).

God does not abandon people who live with mental illness, because God loves us. We are not unlovable because we have a mental illness. Having a mental illness does not disqualify us from experiencing love with God, with ourselves, and with others. In other words, mental illness cannot separate us from the love of God.

Depression cannot separate us from the love of God. Anxiety cannot separate us from the love of God. Posttraumatic stress disorder cannot separate us from the love of God.

When both partners live with mental illness, marriage is especially challenging because the ability to create and sustain a healthy relationship is compromised by the symptoms of the illness. For example, Tom's depression means he has little energy or interest in sexual intimacy. Yoko's PSTD means she feels vulnerable and is reluctant to open herself up to trust Tom when he expresses frustration or anger. When both partners have active symptoms, their intimacy suffers, and their marriage is strained.

What does sustained love look like in Tom and Yoko's marriage? When we consider 1 Corinthians 13, and the description of the power of love, we understand that the love God gives us for our partners helps us to see who the other person is beyond the mental illness. Love invites us to see our partners as beloved children of God. Love says our partner is not their mental illness.

Love says if something is truly a problem for you or your partner, then you both need to do what you can to change it. Love gives us courage to seek help. Love helps us know we are not alone.

Sometimes the mental illness is all we can see, but this is not the whole picture. A person is not their mental illness or their addiction or the worst thing that has happened to them. Love helps us to see the God-image each one of us carries inside of us. Love affirms our worth, value and dignity as children of God. Love and justice are intertwined.

Love is bigger than mental illness. Love is more powerful than mental illness. Love cannot be destroyed by mental illness when love has its faithful foundation in God. God's love is the faithful foundation of the marriage. Marriage is nothing without love. But what happens when the mental illness masks the feelings of love? Or worse, what happens when mental illness steals our love from us?

For marriages like Tom and Yoko's, a mutual commitment to lifelong recovery and treatment help to ground marriage in love. Sometimes love is not even a feeling, it is a promise, it is a daily commitment. Because some days all you feel is sad, tired, worn out, and done.

Marriages affected by mental illness cannot rely on feelings of love alone. At our most difficult moments, feelings of love are nowhere to be seen or felt or found. Love is multi-dimensional and multi-lingual. With God's help, love takes us deeper than we ever imagined possible.

Sometimes love looks like leaving the house so your partner can be alone. Sometimes love looks like going to therapy. Sometimes love looks like taking an antidepressant. Sometimes love looks like going to the gym. Sometimes love means trusting the other person to hold your deepest fears.

Sometimes love looks like getting dressed up and going on a date to a movie. Sometimes love looks like getting naked. But when it comes to marriage and mental illness, love looks like anything it has to, just as long as you recognize it and celebrate it.

Mental illness does strange things to love. We've got to protect our love from mental illness. We've got to put boundaries around mental illness so it doesn't put out the flame of our love. And if mental illness does snuff out the flame of love, then what?

You need to know how to reignite the flame of love and be prepared to do so every day if necessary. You can get help reigniting the flame of love, and you can learn the skills you need for guarding it. You are not alone. God loves you.

Reflection Questions

1. According to 1 Corinthians 13:2, love is something we "have," as opposed to love being something we create. What does it mean to have love in a marriage? Where does this love come from? Why are we nothing without love?

2. How does mental illness such as addiction, anxiety, depression, and PTSD affect the ability to give and receive love in a marriage relationship?

3. Depression is one of the most common forms of mental illness. In what ways can marriage help improve the quality of life for someone living with depression?

Tip for Blessed Unions: Mental Health First Aid

Prepare your marriage for the impact of mental illness by educating yourself on the signs and symptoms of mental illness. Empower yourself with tools and resources to be an advocate for mental health. As a couple, take Mental Health First Aid, a one-day certificate training program offered nationally with the main goal of providing the basic tools needed to respond to a mental health crisis. Imagine a world where central to the premarital counseling experience was a course on Mental Health First Aid. In a blessed union, the marriage certificate and Mental Health First Aid certificate go side-by-side.

Prayer for Love

God of love, you knit us together in our mother's womb and into our being you placed your divine image. You promise to love us, to never forsake us, and to never abandon us.

Breathe your renewing love into our relationships. Give us love from above so we have enough love to get us through the bad days.

Help us to know we are defined by your love above all else and nothing can separate us from your love, not mental illness nor hardship of any kind.

Thank you, God, for your eternal love conquers all fear and even death itself. Your love for us will never end.

Help us to trust in your love for each one of us and to share love with each other. Amen.

Chapter Four:

To Comfort

If I give away all my possessions, and if I hand over my body so that I may boast, but do not have love, I gain nothing. Love is patient; love is kind; love is not envious or boastful or arrogant or rude. (1 Corinthians 13:3-4)

Love is kind. This quote comes from the Bible, but it also could have come straight from my husband's lips. When we first dated, he shared with me how he was looking to be with someone who was kind and how many of the women he dated turned out to be unkind. I was drawn to his own kindness that only deepened as I got to know him. I discovered his kindness came from love. There's no greater sweetness than loving kindness.

Humble and quiet, my husband is not boastful or arrogant. He is a big-hearted and kind man. This is one of the main reasons why I love him. I am drawn to comfort my beloved when I remember that in our marriage, he is God's love made flesh.

On our best days, my husband is God's kindness shown to me. He is God's way of comforting me just as I seek to comfort him. Whether it's a shoulder massage, making dinner for our family, or buying me fresh flowers (as he does every week), my husband shows his love through kindness. Even in the midst of the challenges of mental illness in our marriage, we can still be sources of comfort and love to one another. And on our bad days, these fresh memories of kindness carry me to a new, better day ahead.

I want to introduce you to Alex and Terri. This couple navigated a mental health crisis that emerged after the birth of a child. Marriages experience tremendous change with the addition of family members, whether by adoption or birth, and this influences the mental health of the couple. Alex and Terri's story highlights for us just how powerful self-stigma can be and how stigma creates a barrier to getting the help we need. Self-stigma is when we are ashamed of our own condition. It can foster self-hatred, leading us to neglect ourselves and deny ourselves the care we need. At the same time, we can overcome self-stigma and free ourselves to receive support and care.

The Blessed Union of Alex and Terri

Alex and Terri had celebrated seven years of marriage when we met to talk about their marriage and mental illness. Alex and Terri met in seminary and married after dating for less than a year. Terri was preparing to be a local church pastor when they started dating and Alex was training to be a hospital chaplain. Their wedding took place the same weekend as their graduation from seminary with their Master of Divinity degrees.

Alex and Terri both grew up in working class homes in the Midwest. Their families both had roots in Eastern Europe. Alex and Terri experienced stable childhoods that fostered a healthy sense of well-being. Neither family talked about mental health growing up, and neither Alex nor Terri had significant adverse childhood experiences, apart from some financial stress.

The church was central to both Alex and Terri's lives, providing their families with a sense of belonging and community. Terri knew she wanted to be a pastor since she was a little girl in Sunday school. The story of Jesus feeding the five thousand with loaves and fishes captured her imagination and ever since then she wanted to follow Jesus. Terri's uncle was a pastor, and so she followed in the family tradition.

Alex knew he wanted to be a hospital chaplain ever since he was hospitalized with appendicitis as a freshman in college and the chaplain came to pray with him every night at his bedside. He never forgot the kindness of the gentle chaplain who, more than anything, was a calming presence during a scary time. Alex wanted to be that non-anxious, calming presence for others.

When Alex and Terri got married, they had a combined graduation party and wedding celebration with both sides of the family pitching in to help. Terri's uncle officiated at the wedding. After Alex and Terri's second year of marriage, they welcomed their first child into the world.

Terri experienced postpartum depression with the first child, and with the second child, her symptoms of depression became more severe and long-lasting. After her first child, Terri had felt glad to return to work at the church, so she could think about something else besides the repetitive tasks of baby care. Now with the second child, Terri couldn't imagine having the energy to get back to work so soon. No matter how much sleep she got, she woke up feeling exhausted.

Terri had six weeks of maternity leave from her job as a pastor, but found with her second child, she was not ready to return to work at the church when the time came. Alex figured she was anxious about being separated from the baby, but he started to get concerned when he noticed Terri was no longer showering and hadn't changed her clothes in days. True, she wasn't leaving the house, so some relaxed hygiene was understandable. But something was off—she didn't seem quite like herself.

Terri felt this birth changed her somehow. She wasn't feeling the positive endorphins that she remembered from the first birth. She felt too tired to enjoy the newborn baby suckling her breast. Worse than feeling tired, Terri felt numb. Where was the joy? She felt ashamed that she was not happier. In fact, since giving birth she felt more depressed than ever. When Terri prayed to God to help, she felt as though God was not listening. Where was God? Why did God feel so far away?

Alex decided to talk with his chaplain supervisor about the situation at home with Terri. Alex knew that if things were going to get better, he needed to ask for help. Alex knew it was time to break the silence about mental illness in their marriage. The conversation with his supervisor went well, and it reminded Alex that he had supportive people in his life who cared about him.

Alex knew he needed to talk to Terri next. He said to her, "Terri, I love you and I am proud of the amazing family we have made together. Because I care for you, I am concerned about you. I think we need to ask for some help." It was the hardest conversation Alex ever had in his life. He was so afraid of what Terri would do.

Instead of feeling hopeful and comforted, Terri heard Alex's words through the filter of her depression. She felt scared he would leave her. She felt like a failure. Terri didn't know what to do. She felt hopeless. She felt out of control.

Terri was also afraid for anyone at her church to find out about her mental illness. She didn't like it when Alex talked to her like she was one of his chaplaincy patients he would visit at the hospital. She wanted to be his wife, not his patient. She wanted him to be her husband, not her chaplain.

Alex encouraged Terri to ask the church for an extra week of family leave. Terri felt ashamed, embarrassed, and angry that she was struggling to take care of the baby, let alone take care of herself. She was beating herself up with self-critical thoughts: "Haven't I already done this once before? Shouldn't it be easier the second time? What's wrong with me?"

In the moments when her depression lifted slightly, Terri felt grateful for Alex's support.

Alex picked up the extra responsibility for cleaning, cooking, and caring for their older child while Terri stayed in bed for days at a time. He suggested they tell the doctor what was going on at her next follow-up appointment.

Terri had mixed feelings about possibly going back on her psychiatric medication. She hadn't taken any of her antidepressants since she found out she was pregnant. She now worried that stopping her medications during the pregnancy was a mistake. But she was also afraid the pills would contaminate her breast milk. For a moment Terri wondered if she could replace her medication with prayer and extra reading of the Bible. If she had more faith, would she be cured? She prayed that God would cure her of mental illness.

Could she pray away her depression? Terri worried that God was somehow punishing her for not being a better wife and mother. She felt like a failure at life. She wondered if Jesus' mother Mary ever felt this bad after giving birth to Jesus. The Bible never said anything about it.

After weeks of the situation not improving, Alex and Terri ultimately decided to follow the doctor's advice and seek inpatient treatment for Terri's serious postpartum depression. They both had to fight feelings of shame and fears of financial ruin; the dream of having children was turning into a nightmare because of severe mental illness.

They didn't want to tell the church because they were afraid of the stigma if Terri's congregation knew about her illness. The fear of stigma and rejection by the church was causing Terri to isolate herself. What if the congregation wouldn't want her anymore as their pastor? What if they fired her? What if she lost her ministry forever? Terri decided to not tell the church that she was inpatient for psychiatric treatment during her family leave.

On her discharge from the inpatient program, Terri's doctor recommended that she continue to receive care through a long-term outpatient program. This meant Terri would need to adjust her work schedule once she returned from family leave. She decided to email her church council president, informing him of her medical condition.

When Terri sent the email, she said a prayer. Terri prayed the people in her church would show her compassion and love. Even though she served as the pastor, she was still human just like them, after all. She hoped that her mental illness would not be viewed as weakness, but as humanness.

Terri had provided pastoral care to the wife of her council president a few years before. She remembered standing by the hospital bedside of his wife as she lay dying. She remembered offering her communion and praying the Lord's Prayer with her for the last time. Would this man return the care, compassion, and kindness she had shown his family?

After sending the email, Terri waited anxiously for a reply and checked her email inbox every few minutes. Two days went by without a response.

Then on the third day, this reply came from the church council president:

> Dear Terri: I am sorry to hear you are having a hard time with your new baby. I feel sorry for that baby and wonder if you might consider putting it up for adoption so he can have a loving mother. We are praying for that baby. Send us pictures so we can see him. If you need more time, we guess we can give you more time, but we'll need to deduct pay. Ever since you left, the giving has gone down. People don't think you are coming back.

As Terri read the email, tears of rage welled up in her eyes and her face got hot. She screamed, startling the baby at her breast. Her wails, added to her infant son's, filled the bedroom.

When Alex came home from working his chaplaincy round at the hospital that night, he could tell something was wrong because the house was totally dark, except for the artificial light coming from the television. Terri wouldn't say anything. The baby was sleeping. Their daughter was watching a movie on repeat for what must have been the thousandth time.

Alex sat down on the couch next to Terri, placed his hand on hers and said, "Can you tell me what's wrong?" Terri said flatly, "I quit. There's no chance I'm ever going back to that church. Not after how they treated me. How can they call themselves Christian?"

The trauma of Terri's postpartum depression combined with the treatment by her employer placed a tremendous amount of stress on their marriage. Alex and Terri barely were making ends meet financially, hadn't had time alone together in months, and hadn't seen any friends.

After Terri completed the outpatient program, she and Alex began marriage counseling. They had spent so much time worrying about Terri bonding with the new baby, they had little time or energy to focus on nurturing their relationship as husband and wife. They wanted to experience the comfort of marriage without the disruptions of serious illness, and they needed to work on repairing the bond between them. The spark that once drew them close was gone. Alex and Terri wondered how long a marriage without a spark could last. Their love tank was running on empty.

Alex was patient with Terri's slow recovery, and Terri worked hard at it. With a combination of medication, therapy, and finding a new church in a neighboring town where Terri could serve part-time while she worked on her recovery, things improved. With this weight lifted, Alex and Terri began to rediscover the love that brought them together in the first place.

Despite what happened with the council at her previous church, Terri took a leap of faith and opened up about her mental illness during the interview with the new church, explaining about her successful treatment and recovery. The church leaders welcomed her into the new congregation, believing that her life experiences with recovering from mental illness would make her a better pastor, not a worse pastor. It helped that Kay, the chair of the search committee, was also a woman who also experienced postpartum depression. After Terri shared part of her story, feeling vulnerable and nervous, this created the space for Kay to share her story. The church leaders were impressed with Terri's resiliency, authenticity, and honesty.

In order to support Terri's ministry with them, the congregation offered her an extra day off each month as a "mental health" day so Terri could make her recovery and ongoing mental wellness a priority in her own pastoral leadership. The church saw Terri's leadership and recovery from mental illness as a gift to the community. They felt blessed to have a pastor who could model the journey of mental wellness.

The church also dreamed about doing more to support people with mental illness and their loved ones. They wanted to be a church that welcomed, included, supported, and engaged people with mental health challenges. So, they created a mental health ministry team and began to explore a partnership with a local mental health clinic. They learned that clinic patients often need help getting to appointments, so the team recruited drivers from within the church's membership and set up an on-call schedule and communication system with the clinic. Within a year, the church opened a satellite office on their church campus, which they rented to the clinic's counselors for free. In this way, they were able to make counseling services more affordable and accessible to the neighborhood.

As for Alex and Terri, when asked, they say their marriage is not perfect...but they are learning how to be kind to one another and how to show kindness to themselves. They are weaving together love and justice into their married life. They learned it is lifesaving to ask for help and sometimes love looks like admitting we can't do this alone. Sometimes saving a marriage means inviting others in. Sometimes happily ever after means getting help.

Loving ourselves and loving others with mental illness means we celebrate the support we can give and accept the support we need. There is no shame in needing help. There is no shame in receiving comfort from others. Mental illness doesn't have to stop us from having a blessed union.

Mental Illness: Postpartum Depression

Postpartum depression is a medical condition that occurs in a mother just before or after her baby is born. Most new moms experience "baby blues" after childbirth, which commonly includes mood swings, crying spells, anxiety, and difficulty sleeping. Baby blues typically begin within the first two to three days after delivery and may last for up to two weeks. Postpartum depression is a more severe, long-lasting form of depression that in rare cases can lead to an extreme mood disorder called postpartum psychosis. Symptoms include depressed mood or severe mood swings, excessive crying, difficulty bonding with your baby, withdrawing from family and friends, loss of appetite or eating much more than usual, inability to sleep (insomnia) or sleeping too much, overwhelming fatigue or loss of energy, reduced interest and pleasure in activities you used to enjoy, intense irritability and anger, fear you're not a good mother, hopelessness, feelings of worthlessness, shame, guilt or inadequacy, diminished ability to think clearly, concentrate or make decisions, restlessness, severe anxiety and panic attacks, thoughts of harming yourself or your baby, and recurrent thoughts of death or suicide. **Postpartum psychosis** includes the following symptoms: Confusion and disorientation, obsessive thoughts about your baby, hallucinations and delusions, sleep disturbances, excessive energy and agitation, paranoia and attempts to harm yourself or your baby.

Comfort and Mental Illness

Alex and Terri both stood at the altar and made promises to comfort one another as part of their marriage vows. They were not prepared as newlyweds for the challenges to come that would make providing comfort nearly impossible. How do you comfort a mother who is caring for an infant and feels like she might not survive?

Sometimes all you can do during a serious medical crisis is hold onto your partner's hand and look at them with a loving gaze while professional help is on the way. Try to remember you are deserving of love. You both are. Remembering mental illness is a health condition, just like heart disease, can help to ease the guilt often associated with postpartum depression. Too often we blame ourselves for being sick. Mental illness is not our fault. Mental illness is not a punishment from God.

One of my favorite scriptures is from Psalm 23, and comes right after the "valley of the shadow of death" part: "I will fear no evil for your rod and staff—they comfort me." Even though the idea of using agricultural equipment for comforting doesn't make much sense to us anymore, God is still like a shepherd who guides us through difficult paths, protecting us as we journey through the shadow of death. In Hebrew, the word death more accurately means darkness or shadows. The psalmist knew that our lives would take all of us through valleys of shadows. But we aren't left alone in the shadows, we are not abandoned or forsaken.

God uses the staff with its hooked end to pull us out of ditches. The rod is to fend off coyotes and other predators. God comforts us because God is with us, even in the worst parts of life. It is God's original blessing of comfort that allows us to find comfort for ourselves and then to be able to comfort others.

Offering comfort in the face of mental illness is hard. Stigma and shame challenge us in seeking comfort because they lie to us. They tell us we don't deserve to be comforted. Like Terri, we can believe the lie mental illness tells us: we are not good enough, we are bad, we shouldn't exist, our families would be better off without us. All lies. Finding ways to cope and discovering what brings you comfort in times of mental illness become key to everyday survival.

The promise to comfort our partner is a promise to show love through action. We show comfort through our words, and by what we do and by what we don't do. According to 1 Corinthians 13:4, love means we don't act enviously, boastfully, arrogantly, or rudely.

Living with mental illness is not an excuse for bad behavior, and a partner's mental illness is no excuse to treat our partner badly. Emotional and verbal abuse is sinful, even if the behaviors are caused by mental illness. Mental illness is no excuse for abuse. If you are acting in ways that cause harm to yourself and/or others, please seek help immediately.

Love is patient and love is kind (1 Corinthians 13:4). It can be hard for people living with mental illness to be patient and kind to themselves because of self-stigma. We can cast judgment towards ourselves and blame ourselves for our illness, thinking we are unworthy of love. Why is it so hard to be kind to ourselves? Is it because we know every flaw and every imperfection? Loving ourselves takes patience and kindness.

Part of marriage is the work of strengthening self-love, not only focusing on loving the other person. Many times, we focus on how to comfort others—so much so that we neglect nurturing our own need for comfort. We forget that when we make our marriage vows, we not only promise to be patient and kind to our partner, but we promise to be patient and kind to ourselves. Comfort in a marriage goes both ways.

It takes time, energy, effort, and intention to remember that God wants us to find comfort for ourselves. Comfort is kindness in action. It's what you do for yourself and for others to show you care and that you matter.

Reflection Questions

1. 1 Corinthians 13:4 says, "Love is patient; love is kind." How might mental illness in a marriage challenge and redefine what we think of as patience and kindness?

2. How does the stigma of mental illness create barriers to receiving and giving comfort? How might a congregation care for their pastor's mental health? Offering a monthly "mental health day" in the call agreement is one example—what are some other possibilities?

3. Postpartum depression is extremely common, impacting as many as one in five mothers.[18] Yet, we often do not discuss it. What narratives around motherhood contribute to the stigma of this form of mental illness?

Tip for Blessed Unions: Self-Care

Create a self-care comfort zone in your home. This is a space where you can simply be, without any feelings of discomfort. It might be lying down on the floor or sitting by a window or curling up on the couch. This might be a space you share with your partner, or a place where you can enjoy time alone. The main thing is that in this space, you feel a deep sense of comfort and peace. Sometimes a weighted blanket, heating pad, or soft carpet can help create the physical sense of comfort your mind needs to feel at ease.

Create rituals of comfort. Take time each day to comfort yourself and your partner through rituals of care. This ritual could be serving each other coffee or tea, lighting a candle and naming an intention to be fully present to one another, or a ritual involving loving touch and showing affection. Repeat visits to this self-care comfort zone often. Taking at least twenty minutes for yourself every day helps honor the importance of taking care of our individual mental health needs so we can be healthy in our marriage. Going to therapy and taking meds is good self-care.

Prayer for Comfort

God of comfort, you create us to need one another. Help us to feel your comfort wrap around us like a soft blanket. When we are unable to show comfort to ourselves and to others, have mercy on us.

Thank you for the gift of comforting relationships where we can show love through patience and kindness. Thank you for the blessings of comfort we experience even in the midst of mental illness.

Continue to comfort all who are in pain, especially those whose mental health is not well today. Answer all who cry out to you and offer us your comforting love. Amen.

Chapter Five:

To Honor

Love does not insist on its own way; it is not irritable or resentful; it does not rejoice in wrongdoing, but rejoices in the truth. (1 Corinthians 13:5-6)

One of the deepest ways I can honor my husband is to honor our differences. We are both stubborn and we approach life from different perspectives. This means we often disagree about basic things. The Bible teaches love does not insist on its own way. In our marriage, we have had to learn how to not insist on getting our own way.

Turns out, letting go of getting your own way is hard. One example is our two very different parenting styles. Like many families, we struggle with creating alternatives to electronic screen time. Often, turning on the device is the easiest way to entertain our children. But most parents agree this this can become an unhealthy habit. My partner and I were having conflict over what the specific boundaries around "screen time" ought to look like and the process for creating and adjusting those boundaries. In family therapy, we've learned how to communicate our concerns and how to honor each other's perspectives.

In therapy we go deeper into the "why" of our differences, helping us to understand why we see parenting differently.

Looking at our marriage from a place of honor means the truth of what's best for our family is most likely somewhere in the middle. Rather than striving for an impossible perfection according to one person's opinion, we learn to let go of unrealistic expectations. Rejoicing for us comes when we meet half-way.

I want to introduce you to Taylor and Chris, a couple who show us how unprepared we can be when behaviors associated with serious mental illness, such as self-harming, hit our marriage. In this story, we see how shame can keep us silent about the realities we experience. But even when shame casts a shadow over our marriage, we can find the truth and rejoice in it. To find the truth is to honor the marriage.

The Blessed Union of Taylor and Chris

When I interviewed them, Taylor and Chris had celebrated eight years of marriage. Taylor's grandparents were from Scotland and Chris's ancestry is mostly German. They were both raised in upper, middle-class Christian homes in the suburbs outside of Los Angeles.

So far in their relationship Taylor and Chris enjoyed positive mental health for the most part, with the exception of them both experiencing episodes of situational depression during their college and graduate school coursework. Situational depression is a fairly common experience among college and graduate students, given the amount of pressure they are under to study, pass exams, research, and write papers. When Taylor and Chris graduated, it felt like the clouds lifted. They both found jobs in their fields of study and they knew not everyone was so lucky.

Taylor and Chris got married while Chris was finishing up graduate school and Taylor was newly ordained as a minister. Their luck continued when Taylor was called to pastor a church in the same town as Chris's new part-time job teaching at a community college. On top of new jobs, they heard surprising news: Taylor was pregnant.

Life was full and hectic, but in a good way. Taylor's parents decided to move to be closer to their daughter who would give birth to their first grandchild, so this additional support buoyed the couple on hard days when life felt overwhelming. Even though the stress of graduate school was over, being newlyweds with new jobs carried a new, different kind of stress.

Two years after their first child was born, they had their second child. They could hardly believe their good fortune. Taylor and Chris believed God was blessing them abundantly. Chris enjoyed teaching and they felt loved by the congregation where Taylor served as a solo pastor. It wasn't a perfect church, but it was pretty good, especially for her coming right out of seminary. Things were going so well, in the back of Taylor's mind, she secretly hoped she wouldn't accidentally mess things up by having a mental health crisis.

Taylor started feeling more and more on edge but didn't want to worry Chris by saying anything about her increasing feelings of mental and emotional instability. Taylor also started fantasizing about romantic relationships with people other than her partner and she worried her private obsessions would lead her to make poor choices. Was it okay to think these things if she didn't act on them? Taylor wanted a quick mental escape from the pressures she felt at work and at home and she found fantasizing in this way released some of the tension she felt inside. But she didn't know if this behavior was part of her mental illness, or if this was just part of being human. She felt ashamed and embarrassed by her fantasies, yet she didn't feel she had the willpower to stop them.

Then on the first Sunday of December, Taylor preached what seemed to her like her best sermon yet, based on her favorite text from the Old Testament prophet Isaiah. The scripture says, "They shall beat their swords into plowshares, and their spears into pruning hooks; nation shall not lift up sword against nation, neither shall they learn war anymore" (Isaiah 2:4). Feeling exhilarated by the experience of preaching with passion and feeling like the mouthpiece of God, she headed into a long meeting right after worship with the trustees. The meeting was to discuss launching a new two-million-dollar capital campaign to repair the old church building and replace the steeple. The meeting took a turn for the worse when the chair of the Trustees announced the bad news that the city denied them the permit.

The uncertainty of the timing of the capital campaign along with the enormity of the amount of money they needed to raise began to overwhelm Taylor. As the meeting went on she developed a migraine and felt nauseated and dizzy. Taylor hoped nobody noticed. She closed her eyes. She clenched her fists. She took deep breaths. She rubbed the temples of her forehead. As soon as the meeting ended, she bolted for the door.

When Taylor got home from church, she collapsed onto the couch. Taylor closed her eyes and started to see images of shadows chasing her. In her mind, she ran down a gravel road until she collapsed, hitting her head on a rock. Whatever it was that was coming after her, she was terrorized by the fear of what they would do when they caught her. Taylor's head throbbed. She then drifted off into a deep, disturbing sleep.

When Chris tried to wake Taylor for dinner, she wouldn't budge. Chris let her sleep, figuring Taylor would wake up when she was hungry for dinner. This was much longer than the pastor's usual Sunday afternoon nap.

During dinner while Chris was feeding the kids, they heard Taylor screaming, "NOOOOO! Get away from me!" The shadows were back inside Taylor's mind, but this time she could see they were chasing her with kitchen knives.

Chris jumped up from the dinner table and ran into the family room. Chris didn't know what was happening, but quickly realized Taylor was bleeding. She had cut herself with the pocketknife she always carried, multiple shallow slits down her left arm from her elbow to her wrist. Chris screamed and ran to get towels to wrap her arm and stop the bleeding.

First Chris called 911. Then Chris called Taylor's parents to come over to pick up the kids. The ambulance arrived just as Taylor's parents' car pulled up in front of the house. At the hospital, after waiting in the ER for two hours, Taylor was admitted to the psychiatric unit for self-harming behavior and hallucinations. The whole episode was a shock to Chris, Taylor, and Taylor's parents. This was more than situational depression. This was serious.

It was late Sunday night while Taylor was in the psychiatric hospital, when Chris got a phone call from the doctor who evaluated Taylor. The doctor told Chris that what Taylor experienced is known as an unspecified psychotic disorder.

The psychotic break was so sudden and out of the blue. Taylor walked the white barren hallways of the psych ward, which smelled of bleach and stale Doritos. As she shuffled along in her white institutional slippers, she held her head down low, wondering if this was what it felt like to be possessed by an evil spirit. Was her mental illness some kind of spirit possession? Was God punishing her for unfaithful thoughts? Taylor didn't want to believe it. But part of her wondered if she had been overcome by evil in her moment of despair. Taylor tried again to pray. The only thing that seemed to help was walking. She walked until her feet hurt.

The doctor recommended that Taylor remain in the hospital another day to get more testing and to stabilize her on medications before she could be discharged home. There was also an outpatient program that could help Taylor learn positive coping skills to keep her from destructive behaviors like cutting. Chris and Taylor didn't know what their insurance would cover or if they could afford additional mental health care. The financial uncertainty added stress to an already stressful situation. How could they make the right decision if they didn't know what they could afford?

Early the next morning when Chris came to visit Taylor on the psychiatric unit, they both cried. How could their beautiful lives get to this point? Taylor insisted Chris not tell any of their friends or anyone at the church what had happened. The town was too small, and word would get out. They were both afraid of what people would think. The couple feared losing custody of their children.

Could they take away the kids because of Taylor's mental illness? Even though Taylor's cutting was self-inflicted, if people heard about it, they could start rumors of her turning the knife on Chris, or worse, the children. Taylor never once thought about hurting the people she loved most and the prospect of other people accusing her of this made her feel sick. Yet, she knew the stigma and fear about mental illness caused people like her to be demonized. This is why Taylor wanted to keep her hospitalization private.

Taylor was released from the psychiatric hospital on Wednesday afternoon and attended the church council meeting later that same night. She didn't want to risk losing her job. She casually mentioned that after church on Sunday she got sick for a few days with the flu. Taylor told the church leaders she felt better now, and she wasn't contagious anymore.

Taylor hoped they wouldn't notice how badly her leg was shaking under the table. She wore a loose fitting, black, long sleeve shirt to cover the bandages. Taylor tried to hide the visible signs of her mental illness. She wondered to herself, "Do I look sick? Do I look mentally ill?"

Taylor was disappointed in herself. She couldn't believe she was too ashamed to tell her church the truth. Taylor was angry at herself for not being "strong" enough to handle life. She doubted her ability to be a good pastor. Taylor wondered how she could lie to the church (or at least not tell them what happened) and still be trusted to preach the gospel. She didn't know any other pastors with mental illness, at least no one who admitted it.

The more Taylor thought about being a pastor who also lived with mental illness, the more questions she had. Where were the boundaries between what the church has a right to know and her right to privacy? What was mental illness doing to her and her faith? Seminary did not prepare her for this, she thought.

Meanwhile, Chris was angry for not somehow preventing this episode. Chris wanted to protect Taylor and the kids. Was it Chris' fault? These feelings of anger and resentment began to cast a shadow over the marriage. Hardly perceiving it at first, Taylor and Chris emotionally disconnected from each other. Their doubts and concerns began to build an invisible wall, brick by brick, one worry at a time.

The following Sunday, exactly one week from her psychotic episode, Taylor insisted on being back in the pulpit. Since her last sermon so much had happened. Taylor had been to the psych ward and had given up her handbag with her wallet, phone, and keys in it and all the photos and notes that signified her identity as a partner, parent, professional, and human being. She had stripped down naked to put on a sterile white gown. She received her clothes and belongings back on discharge from the hospital. But her authenticity didn't feel restored. Now, wearing her black clergy robe embroidered with a gold threaded glory cross, Taylor felt like a fake. What would Jesus do? Would Jesus preach as if nothing had happened?

Taylor knew she had been to hell and back, but she didn't feel like she could tell anyone. She felt like the Old Testament prophet Ezekiel walking through the valley of dry bones, only this time, the bones wouldn't live again. This time, there was only the stench of death. It was as if Taylor was walking alone in the valley of the shadows of mental illness. Where was God?

Taylor felt dead inside. She wondered if this was just another side effect of the medication, in addition to the increased appetite, sweating, and trouble sleeping. Taylor felt a heaviness inside, a dread, believing whatever just happened, would happen again. And what if the church found out?

How much longer could she keep her mental illness a secret? Churches are exempt from most of the employment-related provisions of the Americans with Disabilities Act, at least when it comes to ministers. Taylor worried the church could fire her for having a mental health challenge, especially if she became disabled.

Just days before standing in the pulpit to preach, Taylor experienced the worst kind of pain in her life, a deep aching, a falling into an endless pit, like she was pushed into the shadows. Now she was standing in pulpit preaching, feeling like a hypocrite. None of her seminary professors ever taught Taylor what to do the first Sunday you are back from the psych ward, once again preaching in the pulpit.

Torn between fulfilling the image of the perfect pastor who has it all together, and honoring her own humanity, Taylor erred on the side of caution. She only wanted the church to see the parts of her she was proud of and that they would affirm. Taylor hoped God would forgive her. Maybe someday she could tell her story. Maybe one day she could tell her truth from the pulpit.

But not today. As Taylor preached from her carefully prepared manuscript, she looked out over the congregation and saw her husband and their children. Together they created the family she had always dreamed of—until now. Taylor felt protective of them and proud of how hard they had worked, and how far they had come. She felt like the weak link. Taylor and Chris had beautiful children, landed great jobs at a community college and at a vibrant, growing church. It all felt so fragile now.

One more episode and psychotic break and Taylor feared she would lose everything. Chris was also afraid and worried but didn't share those feelings with Taylor. It seemed as if they weren't on the same page anymore. They both thought if they didn't talk about another psychotic episode, then it wouldn't happen. There remained an uncomfortable silence around both the topic of mental illness and how it challenged their marriage. Taylor agreed to keep taking the medications the psychiatrist prescribed to prevent any additional psychotic breaks, but she wasn't going to take time for any further tests, treatments, or therapy. She didn't want to have to explain them to her personnel committee.

Taylor prayed that God would use the pills to heal her brain of the mental illness. She didn't have time to be sick. She hoped the illness would go away. Taylor planned to stop taking the pills as soon as she felt better. It was her prayer every night that God would heal her mind and free her of mental illness.

Taylor found comfort in her faith through spiritual practices she learned in seminary, such as praying through the Psalms. She found God spoke most clearly to her when she read the Psalms. The words of lament and praise, the highs and lows, connected to her own experiences of life. Taylor knew from firsthand experience that life could take her to the mountain top where everything feels alive and then life could take her to the valley where everything feels dead.

Taylor began to accept the spiritual truth that God was present in both the exhilarating parts of life and in the despairing parts of life. She believed God was with her both on her wedding day in the church and on the day she was carried by ambulance to the psychiatric hospital, and all the days in between her best day and her worst day.

Chris also believed that God would help them recover their marriage from the shadows of mental illness. Yet the stress of mental illness weighed heavily on the couple. Chris worried about Taylor keeping everything to herself because it meant Chris had to as well. How long could their marriage sustain such secrecy? Was it healthy to hide this truth about their new reality?

Chris wondered how long it would be until the next psychotic episode. And would it be worse than the last one? Chris worried about Taylor being left alone. What if there was no one else around to call 911? What if Taylor hurt herself again?

Chris and Taylor feared the mental illness would last forever. Neither one of them thought their marriage would be like this.

Yet, they remained committed to each other. Out of this deep commitment to their blessed union, Taylor agreed to begin meeting with a marriage counselor who helped them address their fears and to make plans for a hopeful future together. They trusted God was still going to bless their union, even if their marriage seemed to be overshadowed by mental illness.

Mental Illness: Unspecified Psychotic Disorder

Unspecified Psychotic Disorder is a psychosis caused by changes in brain chemistry and exacerbated by stress with symptoms of radical changes in personality, impaired functioning, and a distorted or nonexistent sense of objective reality. Common symptoms include delusions, hallucinations, disorganized speech, disorganized behavior often leading to self-harm, or other psychotic emergencies needing urgent medical care.

Honor and Mental Illness

1 Corinthians 13:5-6 reminds us love honors and rejoices in the truth. For now, Taylor and Chris are choosing to keep the truth about Taylor's mental health episode private. Chris is honoring Taylor's wishes for her church to not know about Taylor's hospitalization.

One of the challenges of honoring this wish for privacy is it creates a scenario where Chris and Taylor do not receive support from friends and church members who otherwise may have been willing to pray for them, send a get-well card, visit the hospital, or bring a casserole.

Even if Taylor and Chris had been open about it, there's still a possibility they wouldn't have received much support. Mental illness is often referred to as the "non-casserole" disease. Unlike heart disease or cancer, people who are on bed rest for depression or who are in the psychiatric hospital rarely get the same outpouring of care and concern as those with serious physical illnesses. Stigma dehumanizes people, silences people, and makes their pain invisible.

It is possible even if Taylor's church did know, and care, they may have not known what to do or how to be supportive. It's best to treat a person recovering from mental illness just as you'd treat anyone who is recovering from a physical illness or surgery: send a card, say prayers, drop off homemade cookies, offer to help with chores, babysitting, or offer a ride. Most of all, don't pretend the person hasn't been sick. Silence in the face of mental illness is harmful. Acknowledging the person's pain and suffering caused by mental illness is part of what helps the healing process.

Naming the truth about mental illness honors the person. Honor in the Bible is relational. We are to show honor to those we love. Paul says in his letter to the Romans, "Let love be genuine; hate what is evil, hold fast to what is good; love one another with mutual affection; outdo one another in showing honor" (Romans 12:9-10). One way to understand honor is it draws us closer into relationship while shame, its opposite, drives us further apart.

When we show honor to someone, we value and love them just as they are. When we feel ashamed, we sense that if people knew the whole truth about us, they would not love us or value us. What might it mean to "outdo one another in showing honor" when it comes to marriage and mental illness? Perhaps to honor ourselves and our partner is to help create a shame-free marriage where there is no shame about our experiences with mental illness.

Marriages with mental illness can challenge our understanding of what it means to honor your partner, especially when your partner is experiencing distressing symptoms. Likewise, it can be challenging to feel like you are honoring your partner when your mental illness is flaring up and all you feel you can do is stay in bed. You want to go to work, spend quality time with friends and family, and contribute to the smooth running of the household but you feel like you can't move or breathe.

Hearing voices complicates things even more, especially as people of faith. We can wonder, "Is this the voice of God talking to me?" Mental illness can make honoring a faithful understanding of God more complicated, making spiritual support especially important. With a trusted spiritual director, pastor, or another Christian you trust, you can find ways to honor God's still-speaking voice. You can be both a faithful Christian with a relationship to God and a person living with mental illness.

What does honor look like in marriage when you are hospitalized in a psychiatric unit far from home? My friend David Finnegan-Hosey lives with bipolar disorder and wrote a powerful book about his experiences with psychiatric hospitalizations called *Christ on the Psych Ward* (Church Publishing, 2018). In the book, David shares his story of living with a serious mental illness.

Testifying to the chronic nature of his condition, he says, "Today, I am not fixed. I am not cured. The sickness that was in my bones...is with me still (pg. 146)." He goes on to describe how this type of radical acceptance opens the way for healing and wholeness.

David also writes with honesty about the impact mental illness has had on his marriage. In doing so, David demonstrates that couples who accept the reality of mental illness are better positioned to begin taking the steps that honor the journey of healing. Mental illness and marriage can last "as long as we both shall live."

As David explains in his preface, he was able to write his book, in large part, because his wife Leigh honored who he is: a person with a story to tell. Leigh did not try to hide the truth about their marriage. David was able to tell his whole truth about mental illness because of his wife's "mental, emotional, spiritual, and material support throughout this entire process" (pg. viii). When mental illness is part of our marriage, beautiful things can and do still happen. We all have important stories to tell. It is sacred and healing work to listen.

Honoring our partners means honoring what part of their story they want to tell, when they want to tell it, and how they want to tell it. You may have a story of what it was like for you as a patient. But your partner may have a different story about what it was like to come visit you in the psych ward.

Our experiences may differ greatly from our partners' experiences, as do our perspectives, even of the same moment in time. Love means honoring the fact that your truth may not be your partner's truth. If love doesn't "insist on its own way" (1 Cor. 13:5), then love makes space for our partner's truth alongside of our own.

Reflection Questions

1. 1 Corinthians 13:5-6 says love does not "rejoice in wrongdoing, but rejoices in the truth." What happens when we feel like mental illness is causing one or both of us in our marriage to make harmful choices? Should we honor our partner's wishes if, because of symptoms such as hallucinations, we don't think they are based in truth?

2. What does honor look like for Taylor and Chris? When and why might it be honorable in certain situations to remain silent about mental illness? When might we need to break the silence anyway?

3. There is additional stress for couples where a mental illness is resistant to treatment or does not fit any specific criteria for diagnosis. It's important to remember most forms of mental illness are treatable, yet finding the right treatment can be challenging. How can our faith support us during times when the future is uncertain?

Tip for Blessed Unions: Couples Counseling

The longer I work in the field of faith and mental health, the more firmly I believe in the power of preventative care. Too often, we wait until there is a mental health crisis before we seek out professional mental health care. Consider taking a proactive approach to your mental health and your marriage's well-being by connecting with a marriage therapist. Even if it's only for quarterly check-ups, it's a good idea to establish a relationship with a marriage counselor before trouble arises. Ask about sliding scale services that provide reduced fees if you face financial barriers.

Even in a healthy marriage, there are still ways to make it better. Learning communication and other relationship skills with a professional's guidance can help you be prepared if mental illness or other big challenges do become part of your life together. You can also help to decrease the stigma by walking the talk. Having experience with counseling means you can provide a trusted referral if a friend needs help. It might also prompt you to reach out with empathy, better able to recognize when someone who's struggling needs help in the form of casseroles or babysitting. Don't walk the journey of marriage alone. Find a trusted guide to lead you down the paths of healing and wellness.

Prayer for Honor

God of honor, help us to know the truth of your divine love. Show us mercy and forgiveness when we bypass the truth and rejoice in wrongdoing.

May we open our hearts to truly honor the gifts you have given to each one of us. Give us the ability to celebrate the diverse gifts others bring into our lives.

Thank you, God, for the reminder that love can be gentle and doesn't insist on its own way. We are blessed because you desire to be in an intimate relationship with us.

Holy One, fill us with your liberating truth. Make us unafraid to see ourselves and grant us courage to honor your divine image within. May all power, glory, and honor be yours forever and ever. Amen.

Chapter Six:

To Keep

Love bears all things, believes all things, hopes all things, endures all things. Love never ends. But as for prophecies, they will come to an end; as for tongues, they will cease; as for knowledge, it will come to an end. (1 Corinthians 13:7-8)

I keep the ones I love close to my heart. Or at least, I try. It's hard to keep someone close when you feel like running away. Part of what it means for me as a person living with PTSD is when I am triggered, all I want to do is get away, even when it doesn't make sense to do so. I feel this urgent need to remove myself from the situation. I feel in my bones I need to leave. For me, keeping my beloved means working through the impulse to get away. In my own work of healing and recovery, I've learned to sit with these uncomfortable feelings and, as odd as it may sound, to embrace them.

It turns out I do need to run, but not away. I need to run towards these feelings and get deep inside them. In my marriage, one of the ways I experience healing is to stay and keep my beloved close. It's not easy to do, especially when I feel wired to run. But we are working on it one day at a time.

I want to introduce you to Aimee and Mark. The story of this marriage highlights the delicate dance of how to support a partner who is in the midst of a mental health crisis. The marriage relationship is an intimate bond of trust, but what happens when for the sake of safety, a partner has to make a decision on behalf of the other that goes against the partner's wishes?

The Blessed Union of Aimee and Mark

When I interviewed them, Aimee and Mark were newlyweds. Aimee is second generation Korean American and Mark's parents are from England. This is a second marriage for both Aimee and Mark, who met on a Christian dating website.

Aimee and Mark recently moved across the country for Mark's new job as the pastor of a church outside of Orlando. They moved while Aimee was in her last trimester of pregnancy, having lost one previous pregnancy. This was a new start for them both. They felt hopeful about their child's birth, and they expected that Aimee, a nurse, would find work after some time off with the new baby.

Aimee experienced her first psychotic episode while honeymooning with Mark in Greece. Over several days she had felt increasingly agitated and impatient. At one point she refused the taxi ride Mark had arranged and insisted they walk back to their hotel, a dangerous and hot three miles. That evening after dinner Aimee had severe vomiting and declined even the bottled water that Mark offered. Fearing dehydration, he'd taken her to a local hospital. Through the kindness of strangers Aimee and Mark navigated medical care in another language and figured out how to get Aimee home safely.

Once home, Aimee at first refused to see a doctor. She didn't trust the medical care she had received in the hospital since it was outside the United States. She believed her diagnosis of severe dehydration was wrong; that her sickness had actually been caused by food poisoning. Mark hoped she was right. She was a nurse, so perhaps she knew best, Mark thought.

Still, Mark couldn't suppress the urge to search the internet for answers. That's when he saw that Aimee's symptoms mirrored schizophrenia. As he scrolled, he had his first inklings of what it is like to be married to a person with the symptoms of mental illness who denies she has an illness. Everything Mark read on the internet pointed towards a serious brain disorder. Mark felt helpless. He also felt angry with Aimee for not agreeing to get help.

Mark used to wonder how becoming parents would change their lives. Now he wondered how whatever was happening to Aimee would change their lives, possibly forever. Was this mental illness? The symptoms that had landed Aimee in the hospital in Greece had passed, but she still seemed unwell. For one thing, when she would watch television, instead of settling in with her favorite streaming series, she'd click around and spend only a few minutes on random episodes of shows she didn't normally watch. Instead of feeling relaxed after an hour of TV and coming to bed, she'd continue this pattern late into the night, muttering at the screen for hours. She couldn't concentrate; she didn't want to sleep. This was more than "pregnancy fog," Mark concluded. Yet Aimee continued to refuse to see a doctor (other than pre-natal check-ups) and adamantly opposed taking medication while she was pregnant.

Mark noticed that Aimee didn't seem to think there was a problem at all. He worried, "What will happen when the baby comes?" Mark prayed even more fervently, "O Lord, please take this illness from us." Mark's pocket-sized Serenity Prayer card was wearing thin.

Meanwhile, Aimee felt confused about what was happening to her. She had worked hard to get through nursing school, survived an ugly divorce from an abusive husband who cheated on her, and now was head-over-heels in love with Mark. She thought maybe her nerves were getting the best of her because she was trying so hard to not mess things up.

On their honeymoon, Aimee realized she didn't feel like herself. Aimee blamed the heat, exhaustion from trying to navigate the different culture, and most of all the food, which made her violently ill. Mark's kindness, compassion, and gentleness helped Aimee feel that no matter what they faced, he would be there to support her.

Mark's first wife died in a car crash just three months after their wedding. She was driving home from a women's retreat in the mountains. A drunk driver hit her. Ever since her death, Mark promised that if God ever allowed him to fall in love again, he would do whatever he could to protect his new partner. Mark feared Aimee was at risk of dying and didn't want to risk losing her to mental illness. Mark prayed that God would take the mental illness away from his wife. He tried to focus on the good things in his life, like the church he was now pastoring.

Mark's new congregation was excited to welcome Mark and Aimee's baby into the world and planned a baby shower. At the shower, Aimee enjoyed the attention, but Mark worried her mood was starting to swing up too high. Perhaps it was just the joy of the occasion, but Mark had noticed a pattern of mood swings emerging in Aimee, and he was afraid she might swing rapidly back down at any minute. Without Aimee's cooperation, however, what could he do but stand by and hope for the best?

When they arrived home from the baby shower, Aimee was moving around the house frantically. She began to hide the shower gifts around the house so they "wouldn't be stolen." Mark asked, "Who is going to come into our house and steal our baby stuff?" Aimee said, "Didn't you notice the truck? We were followed all the way home from church." Mark didn't see a truck; in fact, there were no other cars on the short drive home.

Aimee then spent the next hour carefully hiding all the baby gifts. She put the diapers in the shower, the bottles of lotions and soaps in the dishwasher, and the newborn outfits behind the cereal boxes in the kitchen pantry. Aimee stuffed the handmade baby blankets under the bed.

When Aimee finished hiding all the baby shower presents, she yelled, "Now we are all set!" Then she climbed into the deep bathtub, surrounded by all the new stuffed animals for the baby.

She put the life-sized stuffed dog on top of her body, hiding her belly from the burglars, too. Her mind raced with this thought: "What if they try to steal my baby?"

After Googling Aimee's symptoms—active hallucinations—Mark realized what his wife was experiencing could be very serious and not just something "inside her head" that would go away on its own. He decided to call Aimee's doctor and tell her what was happening. The doctor asked Mark to bring Aimee to the hospital so she could check and see if she was a danger to herself, her baby growing inside her womb, or others.

Mark drove Aimee to the hospital. After examining her, the doctor recommended for the safety of Aimee and the baby that they stay overnight at the hospital for monitoring. Mark's mind went to the worst-case scenario if the hallucinations didn't stop: his wife would be hospitalized for the remainder of her pregnancy.

Aimee was frustrated with Mark's lack of trust. It's true that she was not feeling like herself, but wasn't that because of the pregnancy? Aimee didn't appreciate Mark's constant nagging and always monitoring her every move. She wished that he would believe her when she said they were being followed.

Why, Aimee wondered, does Mark always have to be right? She began to worry that he might be planning to leave her. Maybe he didn't find her attractive anymore because of the weight she gained and was using mental illness as an excuse. She began to wonder if he was having an affair. While she was in the hospital overnight, what was he doing and who was he doing it with?

Mark felt overwhelmed by Aimee's erratic and bizarre behavior. He wondered if taking Aimee to the hospital was the right thing to do, but he felt it was better to be safe than sorry. The whole situation confused and drained him.

Getting Aimee to the hospital had been difficult. Aimee at first refused to get out of the bathtub so he made up a story about them going to the police station to report the truck she was sure had followed them home. Mark hated that he lied to Aimee. God would understand, Mark hoped.

After Aimee's admission to the hospital, Mark went home alone feeling awful, scared, and heartbroken. He wondered if they would make it. He briefly considered calling his mom to tell her what was happening but decided against it because he didn't want her to worry. Their baby was going to be the first grandchild on both sides of the family, and he didn't want to ruin things for anyone.

As a pastor, Mark knew the promises of scripture. He trusted that God would guide him and his family through this valley of the shadows of mental illness. Yes, he had faith in God. He also had a bunch of questions that the Bible didn't always seem to answer.

What was going to happen next? When he went back to visit Aimee in the hospital, who would he find? Was this the same woman he married? There was so much about the future that was uncertain. Mark wanted to know if there was a cure. He set out to discover some answers.

Mark wondered if maybe God was calling him to use this tragic experience to help others. Mark knew God could take our moments of greatest suffering and transform them so that somehow our pain was not in vain. More than anything, Mark wanted any future sharing of their experiences to be more than just about mental illness. He wanted to be part of finding a solution.

Aimee's hospitalization was a turning point for her, for Mark, and for their marriage. She accepted her diagnosis of schizophrenia. She decided to learn how to live with schizophrenia as a wife and as a mother. Her medications and talk therapy would not make the condition go away, but they would make it manageable, especially when combined with daily self-care habits and time for checking in with her husband. Together, the family dedicated themselves to raising awareness about mental illness and raising funds to support research to find a cure for schizophrenia.

They named their daughter Grace. Mark and Aimee believed it was God's grace that allowed them to continue to love each other deeply, even with serious mental illness in their marriage. Their blessed union showed them nothing could separate them from the love of God, not even mental illness, not even schizophrenia. God is bigger than mental illness.

Mental Illness: Schizophrenia

Schizophrenia is a serious chronic mental illness that typically begins in your early twenties. When untreated it can cause psychotic thinking (impaired perception of reality and ability to communicate), delusions (fixed, false beliefs), or hallucinations (seeing or hearing things that aren't real). Sometimes you don't realize you have a mental illness because of the symptom known as anosognosia (lack of self-insight). Treatment can help with managing symptoms, but most often it is a lifelong chronic illness. There is a lot of success with early treatment, after the first break. Spotting early warning signs can lead to preventing serious mental illness.

Keep Bearing All Things, Even Mental Illness

The promise we make to keep our partner in the covenant of marriage means we will keep them in good times and bad, in mental illness and in mental health. Sometimes it is this promise, and this promise alone, that keeps us in the marriage. But what if the covenant is broken, what if the bond breaks? How do we know when it is time to let go or if it's time to "keep on keeping on"?

Perhaps the only way to keep bearing all things is to do so with as much support as possible. Like Aimee in the bathtub surrounded by stuffed animals, we need to surround ourselves with support. No matter what support looks like, if it is not harmful to yourself or others, we can give ourselves permission to do what feels best. What does support look like to you?

When we treat mental illness just like other physical illnesses such as diabetes or heart disease, we can begin to understand there are treatment and recovery options available. It is important for us to know about the local mental health resources in our community and to engage with them prior to needing them. Do you know who provides mental health services in your local community? Just as you'd add the phone number of your local doctor, acute care hospital, dentist, and insurance provider into your phone or an emergency list at home, you can also find phone numbers for mental health providers and include them in the list.

The best time to seek out the support of mental health professionals is before there is a crisis. Getting to know the providers and services in your area will help you when the time comes for you or a loved one to get help. This too, is what it means to love. We cannot endure all things alone. Sometimes we need professional help in order to endure.

The Bible says we are to approach loving relationships "with all humility and gentleness, with patience, bearing with one another in love, eager to maintain the unity of the Spirit in the bond of peace" (Ephesians 4:2-3). When we promise in our marriage to keep bearing with one another, this includes bearing each other's health conditions. We do not need to bear the burden of mental illness alone. We were never meant to.

As we think about marriage and mental illness, we can be intentional about cultivating humility, gentleness, patience, unity, peace, and love. Perhaps we can keep bearing all things if we set our intention to keep these characteristics as values in our marriage. It takes humility to admit there is a problem. (Although, as we saw with Aimee, sometimes mental illness can cause lack of insight into the self.) It takes courage to reach out and ask for help.

How do we keep bearing with one another in love? If love never ends, then what about mental illness? Does mental illness ever end? The struggle in marriage is to protect it from the negative impacts of mental illness. We've got to find ways to protect our hearts from the stress.

Is it possible for a marriage to outlast a mental illness? Can love outlast mental illness? Or can love at least quiet the mental illness into a soft whisper? How much mental illness, and for how long, can love endure?

We can't see into the future. But we can choose to trust today and hope tomorrow will be a better day. And we can do everything within our power to make our lives better, for ourselves and those we love. For love to never fail in a marriage affected by mental illness means we must be dedicated to our own well-being and the well-being of our beloved. We must be dedicated to keeping our covenant a priority.

In a blog post titled "Will You Marry Me (And My Mental Illness)," Rebecca Chamaa says her husband got to know her first as a person before he learned about her diagnosis of schizophrenia. "By taking the time to get to know me, the seeds of love started to grow for both of us. As they did, my illness became a challenge we decided to endure together. Instead of tearing us apart, my illness helped us grow in the same direction," she says. "We have learned what it is like to live with and try to manage paranoid schizophrenia as a team. Time, treatment, and a commitment to each other have gotten us through the most difficult periods".[19]

Reflection Questions

1. 1 Corinthians 13:7 says, "Love bears all things, believes all things, hopes all things, endures all things. Love never ends." In this scripture passage we might interpret "all things" to mean all the things related to mental illness—the need to change plans abruptly, to be strong in the face of fear, to

perform countless daily rituals just to manage, and so on. Where can couples find hope when this is their daily reality?

2. What does it look like to fulfill the promise to keep those who are beloved close to us, especially during times of suffering?

3. There is significant public stigma around schizophrenia. What common stereotypes come to your mind when you hear the word "schizophrenia"? In the movie *A Beautiful Mind* based on Sylvia Nasar's biography about John Nash, we see some of these stereotypes played out.[20] How does stigma in the media impact our understanding of mental illness and marriage?

Tip for Blessed Unions: Keeping It Real

Keeping it real means honestly talking to each other on a regular basis about what you are thinking and feeling about the relationship. This includes sharing how you are each feeling emotionally, which can be hard. For my part, I would prefer to ignore warning signs of my partner's upcoming depressive episode and just hope it goes away.

Sometimes I want to escape the reality that our marriage includes mental illness. Yet, keeping it real means talking about hard things and admitting to each other when there is a problem. It is important for all of us to have someone we trust to help us in times when we are unable to perceive on our own that we need help. Michelle Newman, the Director of the Laboratory for Anxiety and Depression Research at Penn State University, said in TIME magazine "to pretend it is not happening, that's one of the worst things you can do." Keeping silent is dangerous because in the silence stigma and shame prevail, preventing us from getting the support we need.

It's surprising how difficult making time to talk about the hard stuff can be when our lives keep us busily going from one thing to the next. Then, when there is time for "real talk," we may not have the energy or desire. Physical intimacy is often connected to our emotional intimacy, which comes from spending time together and honestly sharing with our partners.

Some of the symptoms of mental illness can cause us to feel distance from our partners and so it takes intentional effort to nurture the bonds of connection between us. By committing to keeping it real, we strengthen our "love muscles" that give us the strength to create a blessed union that "bears all things, believes all things, hopes all things, endures all things."

Prayer for Bearing All Things

God who bears all things, believes all things, hopes all things, and endures all things:

We thank you for being with us in all things.

We thank you for the promise that love never ends.

We thank you that we do not bear all things alone.

Hold us as we carry our burdens.

Help us to hope and endure.

Bless us as we rest in your never-ending love. Amen.

Chapter Seven:

To Be Faithful

For we know only in part, and we prophesy only in part; but when the complete comes, the partial will come to an end. When I was a child, I spoke like a child, I thought like a child, I reasoned like a child; when I became an adult, I put an end to childish ways. For now we see in a mirror, dimly, but then we will see face to face. Now I know only in part; then I will know fully, even as I have been fully known.
(1 Corinthians 13:9-12)

Throughout the years of my marriage, my partner and I have done a lot of growing up. I was twenty-nine and he was thirty-four when we stood before the altar and placed wedding bands on each other's fingers. In many ways we were like the people in this scripture passage: we "spoke like a child, thought like a child, reasoned like a child." Eventually we "became adults and put an end to childish ways." Well, for the most part. If I am being completely honest, sometimes we still do act childish.

Maybe putting an end to selfish, childish ways is the real message here. Acting like a spoiled, selfish child is not what it means to be faithful to my beloved and for him to be faithful to me. Despite our childish ways, we remain faithful through the growing up years.

To be faithful to my beloved means when things bubble up between us, like arguing about how to manage our finances, or selfish disagreements, we hold onto one another so we can grow past it. In a blessed union, being faithful means holding onto each other through the growing up years, however long it takes. And it might take a lifetime.

I want to introduce you to Raymond and Jacqui. This is the story of a long and faithful marriage between two people who learned how to adjust and adapt to one another's mental illness and disabilities. We learn from this couple that blessed unions that include mental illness can flourish and provide meaningful companionship throughout a person's life. Mental illness need not prevent us from enjoying the benefits of a faithful blessed union.

The Blessed Union of Raymond and Jacqui

When I interviewed Jacqui, her husband Raymond had died. They would have celebrated their 50th wedding anniversary that year. Jacqui and Raymond are both descendants from Africa, though neither one knows the particulars of their country or family of origin because the slave trade severed knowledge of such ties. They are both proud of their heritage, its rich culture, and the resiliency to overcome great individual and collective traumas.

Before Jacqui's husband Raymond died, he lived his whole life with the physical disability of cerebral palsy in addition to having a mild form of autism. Jacqui lived with both a hoarding disorder and obsessive-compulsive disorder. Within this blessed union, both people experienced various kinds of mental illness.

When Raymond and Jacqui first met in high school, neither one knew about the other's illnesses or disability because these were mostly invisible. Jacqui hadn't noticed Raymond's slight limp caused by muscle tightness until their third date when she looked out her window and saw Raymond run up the driveway at her house to pick her up.

Over the course of five decades, Jacqui and Raymond learned how to make space in their marriage for their differences. Whenever things got difficult in their marriage, they both turned to their faith to help get them through the hardest days. They began each day reading the Bible together at the kitchen table while sipping coffee. During the course of their marriage they read the Bible over twenty-five times from beginning to end, including the boring parts.

Raymond and Jacqui liked to keep to themselves mostly, since they were both introverts. Their main source of socializing came from their faith communities. Raymond attended daily mass at the Catholic Church and Jacqui was active in the choir at her African Methodist Episcopal church. Even though they always attended different churches and came from different Christian faith traditions, they considered themselves happily married. They enjoyed living together in the same house they bought as newlyweds, located just across the street from Jacqui's church.

Then one morning Raymond didn't wake up. Jacqui was in shock. He died in bed in his sleep right next to Jacqui. The night before, they had stayed up late watching their favorite show on television. Like every night, she then took a rose bubble bath while he did crossword puzzles in bed, waiting for her to join him smelling like roses.

Jacqui was heartbroken by Raymond's sudden death. She was traumatized by his death in their marriage bed. She slept on the couch ever since. She couldn't tolerate lying in bed without him beside her. She missed Raymond. Many days, she lay on the couch for hours, calling out his name. All she heard in reply was the echo of her own voice.

What made Jacqui the saddest was no longer enjoying the things she used to enjoy. She hadn't touched her Bible since Raymond died. She just couldn't bring herself to read the Bible without him by her side, even though she knew she could use the comfort now more than ever.

As a woman of God, even in the most difficult situations, Jacqui tried to look for reasons to give thanks. She realized that dying in your sleep is much better than dying violently in an accident, as the victim of a crime, or suffering a painful death from illness. The more she prayed about it, she began to see Raymond's quick and pain-free death as a blessing.

Though Raymond rarely complained, he lived with chronic musculoskeletal pain due to his cerebral palsy that continued to get more severe over time. This quick death meant that he was no longer in pain. Jacqui wondered if he would still have his limp in heaven. "Why not," she said, "it's always been a part of him. He's probably running with that limp toward Jesus just like he ran to my door when we were dating!"

After Raymond died, Jacqui's only sister, Libby, invited Jacqui to move out to Arizona to live with her and her husband Lou. Jacqui had always enjoyed her annual visits to her sister's home in the desert and she liked Lou's cooking. They had mastered the art of outdoor living when the weather allowed for it.

Jacqui and Libby shared the same faith and she loved the choir at her sister's church, so she agreed. Jacqui realized she was stuck in a rut and she needed a fresh start, no matter how painful it would be to leave the home she and Raymond shared. But it took months for Jacqui to begin to pack up her house and prepare for the move.

It was physically hard some days for Jacqui to get off the couch, so she didn't. In Raymond's death she felt like a part of herself had died, too. Although she looked forward to moving to Arizona, the thought of leaving the home she and Raymond shared disturbed her. She felt like she was abandoning him.

Grief landed in Jacqui's heart in the strangest ways. Even when she tried to entertain herself by watching old reruns on TV, instead of laughing, she would cry. The tears just flowed, especially when she was in her bubble bath knowing there was no Raymond to smell her rose scented skin.

Jacqui felt sad thinking about leaving her church family. A few of the folks from the church choir would call each week to check in on her. Sometimes she answered, most times she didn't. She wasn't in the mood for talking.

What she did miss since Raymond died was singing in the church choir. They kept asking her to come back to sing. She just wasn't feeling like singing, though. She was afraid she'd start crying in the middle of a choral anthem and not be able to stop.

As Jacqui thought about starting over her future life in Arizona, she didn't think she could leave her church, since the people were like her family. She didn't want to leave anyone or anything behind. Jacqui kept thinking, "How am I going to move my whole life to Arizona?"

Besides that, the house was jam packed with things Jacqui had collected over the span of her life. There were piles of books, papers, newspapers, unopened mail, magazines, boxes of assorted items and clothes covering every inch of the house, from floor to ceiling. Raymond and Jacqui had just stepped over or climbed on top of things to get around the house.

Instead of arguing with Jacqui about cleaning up and organizing, Raymond at some point just started to pretend that nothing was wrong. After a while, they both got used to living this way. They never had anyone over to the house, so there was no pressure to change. Any socializing they did happened at church, at other people's homes, or at restaurants.

Jacqui always made sure the clothes they wore out of the house were clean, washing them every night by hand since their washing machine had been broken for years. Raymond always wore the same thing every day: white button-down shirt and navy slacks. Raymond liked to iron everything himself, including his socks. He found this ritual soothing.

Jacqui tried to manage her compulsions, but she felt better if she checked the front and back doors every half hour to make sure they were still locked. Both Raymond and Jacqui knew that checking to make sure things were just the way you wanted them to be was an important part of their life together. Some may call this obsessive-compulsive disorder, but to them, it was just the way things had always been.

After talking to Jacqui on the phone to find out how plans for the move were coming along, Libby began to wonder how well Jacqui would adjust to living with them in Arizona. Libby thought about what it would be like to live with her sister again, now that they were grown women. She also knew about Jacqui's hoarding. Libby said to her husband that night, "You know I love my sister. But once she gets here, she is going to have to change her ways. There is no way we are going to let her turn this place into a rat's nest."

Long ago Libby realized that her sister, and Raymond, too, lived with untreated and undiagnosed mental illnesses. Libby never said anything because she didn't want to intrude. She reasoned, "If they are happy together, why should I interfere?" But now with Raymond gone, Libby started to see herself as her sister's caregiver and this new role empowered her to break the silence about the mental illness in the family.

In the days leading up to Jacqui's move to Arizona, Libby reached out to the local chapter of NAMI and discovered they had a free weekly support group for families whose loved ones lived with mental illness. This support group met at the church right by her favorite coffee shop, so she decided to go to a meeting the following Tuesday night. This was a big step for Libby, acknowledging there was a problem in their family.

Libby was pretty sure she wouldn't adopt the same ways of being faithful in her love for Jacqui that Raymond had. However, she knew she would have to be flexible and possibly learn some new habits of her own. She hoped that living with Jacqui would be joyful but acknowledged that manageable might have to be good enough, at least on some days. If Libby was going to love her sister the best way she knew how, she wanted to know more about mental illness. Love propelled her to expand her understanding of how mental illness impacted relationships, especially in a shared household. Love led her to reach out and seek professional and peer support as a family member impacted by the mental illness of a loved one.

The truth is, mental illness not only impacts the people inside the marriage, it impacts the entire family system outside the marriage as well. Taking steps for mental wellness within a marriage benefits the whole family system, extending out to the wider social network. It turns out that a blessed union which strives for mental wellness helps support a blessed family system. That's a lot of blessings to go around.

Mental Illnesses: Autism Spectrum Disorder, Hoarding Disorder, Obsessive-Compulsive Disorder

Autism Spectrum Disorder is a mental health condition related to brain development that impacts how a person perceives and socializes with others, affecting communication and behavior. Common symptoms include social interaction and communication challenges, sensory issues, repetitive behaviors, and restricted interests.

Hoarding Disorder is the health condition where parting with possessions causes stress and anxiety leading to excessive collection of items because of perceived value and need to save them. Hoarding often creates cramped living conditions, such that homes may be filled to capacity, with only narrow pathways winding through stacks of clutter. Countertops, sinks, stoves, desks, stairways, and virtually all other surfaces are usually piled with hoarded items. And when there's no more room inside, the clutter may spread to the garage, vehicles, yard, and other storage facilities. Hoarding ranges from mild to severe. In some cases, hoarding may not have much impact on your life, while in other cases it seriously affects your functioning on a daily basis. Common symptoms include excessively acquiring items that are not needed or for which there's no space, persistent difficulty throwing out or parting with your things regardless of actual value, feeling a need to save these items, and being upset by the thought of discarding them, building up of clutter to the point where rooms become unusable, having a tendency toward indecisiveness, perfectionism, avoidance, procrastination, and problems with planning and organizing.

Obsessive-compulsive disorder (OCD) is a health condition involving frequent patterns of upsetting thoughts and fears (obsessions) that cause anxiety. When you have OCD, you tend to repeat behaviors, doing things over and over (compulsions) to try to control your thoughts and anxiety. These interfere with daily life and cause significant distress. Common symptoms include fear of being contaminated by touching objects others have touched, doubts that you've locked the door or turned off the stove, intense stress when objects aren't orderly or facing a certain way, images of hurting yourself or someone else that are unwanted and make you uncomfortable, thoughts about shouting obscenities or acting inappropriately that are unwanted and make you uncomfortable, avoidance of situations that can trigger obsessions, such as shaking hands, and distress about unpleasant sexual images repeating in your mind.

Faithfulness and Mental Illness

In some ways, when both partners in a marriage live with mental illness it can be easier to live with one another. There can be a shared experience of the everyday reality and a common understanding within the couple that "things for us are different." There can be less pressure and less expectation about the way things ought to be and this can be comforting. There is no illusion of perfection. There is an acceptance of the way things are and of each other. Peace comes when we accept the things we cannot change.

In the Bible, faithfulness happens in relationship. We are faithful to God, to ourselves, and to others. And even more so, God is faithful to us. The Bible says God is "merciful and gracious, slow to anger and abounding in steadfast love and faithfulness" (Psalm 86:15). From a Biblical view, faithfulness is God's commitment to keep loving us.

Faithfulness does not mean perfection. Faithfulness in marriage means we do our best to live in relationship with our partner and to love them as we love ourselves. Some days we will fail in our relationships. Some days we fail ourselves. Having an extramarital affair is an extreme form of unfaithfulness, but this and less-extreme forms become tempting when we are disheartened. For example, we might put our work, our hobbies, our family, or friends before our partner. Faithfulness in marriage is a daily commitment and we can start again and renew this commitment to be faithful each day.

Faithfulness in marriage when both partners experience mental illness can mean that, over the course of a long marriage, new mental health challenges arise over time. The experience of aging itself exposes us to various mental health concerns, which can be mild or severe. Our physical health changes as we age and our mental health changes, too.

Faithfulness also means being faithful about taking care of your own needs. As one couple shared, in an article in Cosmopolitan magazine titled "What Caring for a Spouse with Mental Illness Taught Me," "Caretakers have a really tough time balancing the needs of their spouse with their own needs. Eventually, with the help of some pretty intensive therapy of my own, we were able to find a way to connect. It took about a year to regain footing."[21] Faithfulness in marriage with mental illness is a slow crawl, not a race. It's a zigzag, not a straight line.

Faithfulness may look different for different couples. For some marriages that last into twilight years, mental health challenges pose a risk to physical safety. For example, when one partner has severe dementia, moving the loved one into a memory care unit might be the most faithful thing to do. It's difficult to judge from the outside what faithfulness looks like within another person's marriage, for we cannot truly know the intricacies of other people's intimate lives.

Reflection Questions

1. 1 Corinthians 13:12 says, "Now I know only in part; then I will know fully, even as I have been fully known." When a mental health condition impacts our cognition or our ability to remember, can we still say, "then I will know fully, even as I have been fully known"?

2. What does faithfulness to your partner in the midst of mental illness mean to you?

3. It can be difficult to understand why someone with a mental illness doesn't just "snap out of it" or "get their act together." Especially with hoarding disorder, which can have a negative impact on the hygiene and health of the whole household, we may wonder if the person with the mental health condition loves themselves or loves their family. How can untreated mental illness interfere with the quality of life within a marriage?

Tip for Blessed Unions: Circle of Support

The National Alliance on Mental Illness (NAMI) is the nation's largest grassroots organization providing education, advocacy, and support to people living with mental illness and their loved ones. Most every city and many counties have a NAMI chapter and they provide free support groups, including Peer-to-Peer and Family-to-Family formats. Getting support for yourself and your loved ones from people with firsthand, personal experiences with the challenges of mental illness can help you navigate one of life's most difficult valleys. And the best part: you know you are not alone.

Prayer for Faithfulness

God who is faithful, we trust in time all truth will be revealed. We do not always understand why things happen as they do. Yet we place our trust in you.

Thank you for the promise that we will see you face to face. We praise you for your faithfulness to us and for your presence with us even when we may not be able to see you.

Bless us with faithfulness in our promises we make to love others and to love ourselves. Pour out your grace into our lives and do not hide your face from us. Amen.

Chapter Eight:

As Long As You Both Shall Live

And now faith, hope, and love abide, these three; and the greatest of these is love. (1 Corinthians 13:13)

I don't know how long I will live. Do any of us? When it comes to living out the remainder of my days, I hope for a few things. One of my greatest hopes is to see my son grow into a flourishing adult, finding peace and joy in this life in whatever way makes sense to him. And when I think about my son growing up, I want his father and me to be in the picture with him. Part of navigating our marriage is figuring out what it means to be parents in the midst of our own mental health challenges (let alone the significant challenges that come with parenting itself). I want my child to know mental illness is something that can be treated. Caring for the mental health in our marriage contributes to the mental well-being of our whole family.

In the traditional marriage vows each member of the couple affirms their promises will stand "for as long as we both shall live." But maybe it would make more sense to say, "for as long as we both give each other life." What if, in our vows, we placed the emphasis on the marriage being "life-giving" instead of potentially draining the life out of us until we dwindle down to nothing? My partner and I have decided that if there are more good days than bad, for us that is enough. Under these conditions we hope our marriage will last as long as we both shall live. The irony is, even though we promise lifelong commitment to each other as part of our vows, no one is promised more good days than bad in our marriages.

I want to introduce you to Luis and Gina. This is the story of a blessed union where mental illness created stressful dynamics that strained the relationship to the breaking point. I don't judge or invite others to judge couples who choose to end their unions, because each couple's story is unique. This story also contains the difficult example of death by suicide.

According to a special edition of TIME magazine published in 2019, among the age ten to thirty-four population, suicide is the second leading cause of death. Despite impacting millions of people, suicide is one of the topics least talked about. This story invites us to think about blessed unions impacted by this tragic outcome of serious mental illness. You have permission to skip this story if discussion of suicide is triggering.

The Blessed Union of Luis and Gina

When I interviewed Gina, she and Luis would have celebrated fourteen years of marriage. Luis and Gina are both first generation immigrants from South America and practice the Christian faith. Luis was diagnosed with bipolar disorder in high school and began what would become a lifelong treatment and recovery program. Gina lived with an eating disorder that started in elementary school when her breasts began to develop before the other girls her age.

Luis and Gina were high school sweethearts and married a week after college graduation. They both loved God and believed that God brought them together. Luis and Gina both believed that God uses science to help bring healing in the form of medications. But throughout their marriage even though Luis faithfully took his medication and was in therapy, he was hospitalized multiple times for engaging in suicidal behavior.

Although Luis did everything his doctors told him to treat his mental illness, he still could not get rid of the intrusive thoughts of suicide. He lived with these thoughts inside his head every day of his life. Most of all, he wanted the physical and mental pain of his mental illness to go away. Luis and Gina prayed every day for a cure.

Early in their marriage, Luis and Gina agreed they wouldn't have any children. Luis didn't think he could be a good father and Gina didn't think she could be a caregiver to both Luis and a baby. Plus, Gina's eating disorder caused her to fear what pregnancy might do to her body. She liked to control how she looked, weighing herself twice a day, following a highly regimented diet, and exercising for two hours every morning at 5:00. She would often skip meals to help keep the scale at the perfect number:100.

However, as she got older Gina began to rethink her decision to be childless. More of her friends started having babies. As she entered her early 40s, she felt new urges to become a mother. It was as though the urges grew from inside of her.

Gina stayed up late at night imagining how she would redecorate the study in their small apartment and turn it into a nursery. She tried to drive these thoughts out of her mind, but they drifted back in. At the store, walking down the street, everywhere she went, she suddenly saw babies all around her.

One morning she got up the courage to ask Luis if he would reconsider his decision to be child-free. It had been over a year since his last engagement with suicide and hospitalization. Luis remained firmly against having kids. He was afraid the mental illness would haunt future generations. The one thing he could control was to simply not spread the disease by having children.

When Luis and Gina had exchanged their marriage vows on a sunny autumn day, standing in front of the altar, they said yes to being each other's beloved "for as long as you both shall live." And they meant it.

Luis wanted to honor Gina and to respect her desire to have a child. Gina wanted to honor Luis and to respect his decision not to have children. Yet they began to seriously question whether or not their blessed union was going to last as long as they both would live. They began weekly marriage counseling sessions with the hope of saving their marriage.

Luis was afraid of losing Gina, but he was even more afraid of losing himself. He did not want to parent while having a severe mental illness, and he couldn't get past his fear of passing along the illness to their child.

Gina was afraid of missing out on her one chance at being a mother. In her dreams, she could see herself holding a baby. Why would God give her this dream if God didn't want her to have a baby, she wondered. Gina confessed she wanted someone to hold onto and someone who would always love her if Luis died.

Therapy did not change Gina's longing to have a baby. She discovered that for her, love meant ending the marriage with Luis and finding a way to have a baby. After a year of marriage counseling, she filed for divorce. She was tired of living a life she didn't want anymore.

Luis and Gina's love for each other did not change. Was their marriage over because of mental illness or because of something else?

Two years after the divorce was finalized, Gina remarried. Luis never remarried and later tragically died by suicide. When Gina found out about Luis' death through mutual friends, she was heartbroken. She felt guilty and wondered if staying married would have saved him.

Luis was her first true love. She wondered if the suicide was her fault. Yet, in a counseling session, her therapist reminded her though suicide is preventable, sometimes we cannot know why it is people's lives end this way. No one killed Luis. He died from mental illness. Just like how people die from cancer. Mental illness can be a deadly disease.

The therapist assured Gina the suicide was not her fault. It happened because it was the only way at that particular moment in time that Luis knew how to stop his pain. Death by suicide is often caused by an uncontrollable impulse. Grieving the death of a loved one by suicide is especially complex because there will always be more questions than answers: Could I have stopped it? Did I cause it? Is it my fault? Why did it happen? How could this happen to me, to them, to us?

Though Gina found joy in her new marriage, part of her always ached for Luis, wishing he was still alive. Gina found comfort in lighting a candle in honor of his life every year on the anniversary of his death. Nothing, not even death, could take Luis from her heart.

Can a marriage that has ended in divorce still be a blessed union? The story of Luis and Gina shows us the answer is yes. The marriage they shared still reflected God's love for them both. Choosing to end a marriage does not end God's love for you. Even death cannot separate us from the love of God.

Mental Illness: Bipolar Disorder, Eating Disorder, Suicide

Bipolar Disorder is a mental health condition that causes major mood swings from feeling high and energetic to feeling very low, sad, and hopeless. The periods of highs and lows are called episodes of mania or hypomania (lower grade of mania) and depression. A bipolar disorder diagnosis puts you at a higher risk for addiction. Common symptoms of mania include feeling abnormally upbeat, jumpy or wired; increased activity, energy or agitation; exaggerated sense of well-being and self-confidence (euphoria); decreased need for sleep; unusual talkativeness; racing thoughts; distractibility; and poor decision-making—for example, going on buying sprees, taking sexual risks or making bad investments. Common symptoms of depressive episodes include depressed mood, such as feeling sad, empty, hopeless, or tearful; irritability; marked loss of interest or feeling no pleasure in all—or almost all—activities; significant weight loss when not dieting, weight gain, or decrease or increase in appetite (in children, failure to gain weight as expected can be a sign of depression); either insomnia or sleeping too much; either restlessness or slowed behavior; fatigue or loss of energy; feelings of worthlessness or excessive or inappropriate guilt; decreased ability to think, concentrate, or make decisions; thinking about, planning, or attempting suicide.

Eating Disorder is a health condition related to persistent eating behaviors that negatively impact your health, your emotions, and your ability to function in important areas of life. The most common eating disorders are anorexia nervosa, bulimia nervosa, and binge-eating disorder. Most eating disorders involve focusing too much on your weight, body shape, and food, leading to dangerous eating behaviors. These behaviors can significantly impact your body's ability to get appropriate nutrition. Eating disorders can harm the heart, digestive system, bones, and teeth and mouth, and lead to other diseases. Common symptoms include skipping meals or making excuses for not eating, adopting an overly restrictive vegetarian diet, excessive focus on healthy eating, making your own meals rather than eating what the family eats, withdrawing from normal social activities, persistent worry or complaining about being fat and talk of losing weight, frequent checking in the mirror for perceived flaws, repeatedly eating large amounts of sweets or high-fat foods, use of dietary supplements, laxatives, or herbal products for weight loss, excessive exercise, calluses on the knuckles from inducing vomiting, problems with loss of tooth enamel that may be a sign of repeated vomiting, leaving during meals to use the toilet, eating much more food in a meal or snack than is considered normal, expressing depression, disgust, shame, or guilt about eating habits, eating in secret.

Suicide: According to the National Institute of Mental Health, suicide is the 10th leading cause of death in the United States (the second leading cause for youth aged 10-14; the second leading cause for people aged 15-34; and increasing among the elderly as well).[22]

Men are four times as likely to die by suicide as women because men use more lethal means such as firearms. Women engage in suicidal behaviors at a higher rate than men. On the whole, suicide rates are rising. Measures can be taken to prevent suicide, and risks can be minimized by recognizing warning signs. Warning signs of suicide include changes in behavior, talking about or writing about death and dying or suicide when these actions are out of the ordinary, making comments about being hopeless or helpless or worthless, expressions of having no reason for living or any purpose in life, increased alcohol or drug use, withdrawal from friends or family or community, engaging in reckless behavior or risky activities without thinking, dramatic mood changes, giving away prized possessions, putting affairs in order or tying up loose ends. Common risk factors include losses or other events (such as breakup or divorce, legal, academic, job or financial difficulties), previous suicidal behavior, history of trauma or abuse, keeping guns in the home, chronic physical illness and pain, exposure to suicidal behavior of others, history of suicide in the family.

National Suicide Prevention Lifeline: 1-800-273-TALK (8255) has trained counselors available 24/7 and can refer you to local resources.

Suicide and Mental Illness

Death by suicide is one of the most common forms of death, yet when it comes to talking openly about the enormous amount of suffering suicide causes loved ones, we are silent. Many marriages end in suicide, yet we don't acknowledge it. Stigma and shame associated with this form of death isolates grieving loved ones and complicates their grieving.

In the Bible, the poetry of the Psalms speaks to God loving us as long as we shall live. God's love is with us from the beginning:

"Your eyes beheld my unformed substance. In your book were written all the days that were formed for me, when none of them as yet existed" (Psalm 139:13-16). And God's love will be with us through to the end; not even death can separate us from the love of God (Romans 8:38).

Even though God's love is with us in life and in death, when life ends in suicide, we question how God could have allowed it. We try to understand the reasons why and we fall short. What we can do now is work to prevent suicide and to help people recover from its impact. Breaking the silence about mental illness helps to prevent suicide.

Sometimes even though all the protective measures are taken, we cannot save every life. Yet, it is still important to try. One way is to be trained and certified in Mental Health First Aid, as mentioned in Chapter Three. This training helps you learn the warning signs of a mental health crisis and how to respond.

Blessed unions impacted by severe and chronic mental illness have a higher divorce rate. The multiple stress factors of the medical condition make it difficult to keep the marriage going. As behaviors deteriorate, becoming self-destructive, and moods swing, the relationship suffers. Sometimes even though the love is there, over time the will to continue with the marriage is depleted.

Rachael Keefe is a pastor, married, and lives with mental illness. In her book, *The Lifesaving Church*, she writes about what her mental illness has taught her about marriage and herself. She says, "I learned that it is impossible to love someone enough for them to love themselves." Her first two marriages ended in divorce and she reflects on the reasons why by saying, "I was unable to heal their brokenness, brokenness they were unable to acknowledge in themselves...it took me years to understand that my love alone was not enough to save them from themselves, their own pain—their psychache" (*The Lifesaving Church*, pg. 21).

On a similar note, another writer, Diane, shared in a blog post, "When you live with someone who is mentally ill, the whole environment becomes a bit ill but because you're so 'in' the situation you don't realize how unhealthy it is." Indeed, the glimpses of normality Diane used to get from her friends have largely disappeared. "That's the hardest part," she explains. "The danger of living with a mentally ill spouse is that you lose sight of normalcy and get sucked into the chaos."[23]

Mental illness is not an automatic death sentence for your marriage. Still, it helps to be realistic about how chronic mental illness might affect your marriage "until death do us part." As we age, our symptoms change and the treatments that help will shift. Medications that once worked no longer work. Therapists move away. Resources get drained. Having a long-term mental health plan for your marriage will help support you in fulfilling the promise of "for as long as we both shall live."

In honest and real talk about mental illness and marriage, we can ask these questions: What happens when faith, hope, and love are all affected by mental illness? How can marriages with chronic and severe mental illness last "as long as you both shall live?" Should there be a clause in the marriage vows saying, "unless you have a severe and chronic mental illness"? Is it wise to make this kind of promise in the face of an unknown and uncertain future?

Reflection Questions

1. 1 Corinthians 13:13 says, "And now faith, hope, and love abide, these three; and the greatest of these is love." What kind of support does your community offer to people in blessed unions where there is severe and chronic mental illness?

2. If a blessed union ends either because of divorce or death by suicide, can it still be remembered as a blessed union? Why or why not?

3. When a marriage ends by suicide, we are left with unanswered questions. We wonder if there was something we could have

done to save them. Rachael Keefe says, "The tragedy of suicide is often that the one who dies by suicide does not know that they are causing lifelong pain and grief for those who love them. In fact, the one who dies by suicide often believes that they are sparing their loved one pain." What are some ways faith communities can offer comfort to those experiencing pain from losing a loved one to suicide?

Tip for Blessed Unions: Hold onto Hope

There are days that are hard. There are days when the shadows in the valley of mental illness seem impossible to emerge from unharmed. We carry the scars of our deep love and the great disappointments of love. We hold onto hope because otherwise we lose ourselves in the shadows.

We hold onto hope as an act of resistance to stigma and shame of mental illness. We hold onto hope for ourselves, our loved ones and all who live in the shadows. Hope shines a light into the shadows. Hold onto hope for those who cannot.

In a special edition of TIME magazine on mental health, Joshua Gordon, director of the NIMH said, "Often people who are struggling with mental health issues will be hopeless. Sometimes it is helpful to say 'I know you don't have hope, but I have hope for you. Let me help you.' Hopelessness is actually part of the illness; it's not part of reality." The beauty and power of community is we can be surrounded by other people who hold the hope for us, when we are unable to hold it for ourselves. The power of communities holding onto hope is transformative. This is what faith communities are born to do.

Prayer for Life Eternal

God who loves us as long as we shall live and into life eternal, you promise to love us all the days of our earthly life. Thank you for the gift of marriage and the opportunity to love one another as you have loved us.

We pray for blessed unions that end because of divorce or death. Grant those who grieve and mourn an abundance of mercy.

Send your peace to us now as we seek to fulfill the promises we have made in this life.

As long as we shall live, may we continue to praise you, finding reasons to be grateful for the gifts, large and small, you have given to us. For the gift of life eternal, we give thanks. Amen.

Chapter Nine:

Blessed Union

What is blessed about a union marked by mental illness? How can a marriage impacted by mental illness be a blessing? God blesses every part of our being, even the parts we are too ashamed to mention. Mental illness, like any other health condition, can be blessed by God. God can take our health conditions and bless them by granting us strength to endure, courage to persevere, and hope to overcome despair.

As we know, living in a marriage with mental illness can be painful, disorienting, and isolating. Ways to flourish in a marriage with mental illness include all the tips mentioned thus far, such as educating yourself, finding support, communicating with your spouse, and seeking professional help. One additional tip I'd like to mention is creating a Wellness Recovery Action Plan (WRAP). The WRAP is a self-awareness tool that helps you identify what makes you feel healthy and stable and what causes you emotional discomfort.

Linda Meyer is a wife and mother who has experienced multiple psychiatric hospitalizations. She often disassociated, losing track of who she was, where she was and what she was doing. Linda says her life and marriage was saved by a WRAP, noting in *Oprah* magazine, "My family knows that if I'm driving around and not answering my phone, it's not a good sign because it might mean I'm dissociating. The plan gives them specific ways to help me: My husband might take me out for a drive, or one of my kids might order my favorite Chinese food. They're small things, but for me, they're enough to keep me out of the hospital" (After 5 Suicide Attempts, *O: The Oprah Magazine*, December 10, 2018). These and other proactive steps are essential to ensuring you and your partner have the emotional and practical resources you need in order to heal while nourishing your relationship. I've listed some helpful resources, including a link where you can learn more about WRAP and download a sample template for crisis planning, at the end of the book.

Our marriages can be blessed even when they carry the weight of mental illness. We can know the joy of love even in the midst of the sorrow of mental illness. Medications can help treat mental illness and there is no shame in needing help to adjust our brain chemistry.

Our brains can change over time. Medications need adjustment because they can stop being effective. Perhaps a new wedding anniversary tradition could become getting an annual "check up from the neck up" to test and make sure our mental health is in a good place. As one friend shared, with the guidance of his doctor, "My husband upped his dose of antidepressants and I am beginning to see glimpses of the man I love!"

People living with mental illness and their loved ones are worthy of being part of healthy, loving, life-giving relationships. Mental illness cannot separate us from the love of God. Mental illness does not prevent us from being blessed in our unions.

We can have mental illness in our marriages and at the same time have a healthy marriage. It sounds strange, doesn't it? What I have learned in my own marriage is that having a mind that feels broken sometimes does not mean the marriage is broken, too. Marriages with mental illness can be whole, life-giving, and blessed.

Breaking the silence about mental illness and marriage is an ongoing act of discipleship. We tell these true stories about mental illness and marriage because in liberating them from silence we are healed from the stigma and shame that oppresses us. In sharing our true stories, we realize we are not the only ones. This, too, is a blessing.

My friend Simon, whose wife lives with bipolar disorder, shared with me about the hope that was starting to emerge from his marriage after years of strain. He said, "Beginning to see glimpses of a woman I barely recognize—the woman I married. Joy, laughter, energy. That this is so startling and foreign and so good to me is making real the depths to which we have been over these past weeks and months. After walking for so long in the shadows, I now see a light at the end of the tunnel, making me squint because of how dark and long the walk through the tunnel really was . . . I now understood both the light and the darkness. I am grateful."

While we are not the first ones whose blessed unions contain mental illness, we can be the last ones to keep such truths about our lives a secret. We can break the cycle of silence about mental illness and set ourselves free to do the work of healing and recovery. As Harville Hendrix says, "Healthy marriages lead to healthy homes, which lead to a healthy society" (*Making Marriage Simple*, pg. 147). Breaking the silence about mental illness creates the foundation for mental health justice for all. This is good news.

While writing this book I began to wonder what it might look like to create marriage vows with the intention of making space for the reality of mental illness. How would our promises change if we knew we would be promising ourselves into a marriage with mental illness? What might it look like to break the silence about mental illness and marriage at the altar?

These wonderings led me to create a set of simple marriage vows that can be used and adapted either for a wedding ceremony or for the renewal of vows. It could be a powerful testimony for a couple to renew their marriage after coming out of an especially difficult season of mental illness. Inviting family and friends to witness your renewal of your marriage vows can be a way to break the silence about mental illness and marriage.

A New Vow for Marriage

This is my promise to you:

> I will see you as a whole person, and not as your worst symptom.

> I will love you for who I know you to be, and not for how you feel or behave.

This is my promise to me:

> I will see myself as a whole person, and not as my worst symptom.

> I will love myself for who I am known to be, and not for how I feel or behave.

This is my promise to us:

> We will seek support from family, friends, and wider circles of care so we can faithfully fulfill these promises.

We will bless our marriage each and every day knowing God is love and trusting God is with us.

Tip for Blessed Unions: Embrace the Big Blessed Love

No matter what state our blessed union is in, there is what I call "the Big Blessed Love" that never fails. Each day we wake up to this big love and we can choose to ignore it or to embrace it. All love we experience comes from this bigger source. And the supply of love is endless.

What if we began each day by embracing this Big Blessed Love that is all around us? In our own blessed unions, the positive energy flow may be temporarily blocked because of symptoms of mental illness. That is why it is important to be able to connect to the original source of this life-giving energy. We can take comfort in the fact that love comes from God and comes in an endless supply. Finding ways to fill our spiritual, emotional, and marital lives with this positive, life-giving energy becomes the opportunity we have before us.

Big Blessed Love moves us out of our small selves and gives us the energy to invest in our blessed unions. Big Blessed Love comes from God and God's love never fails. When experiencing mental illness within our marriages, embracing the Big Blessed Love can sustain us on those long and lonely nights. God will not leave us heartbroken. God's love heals.

Prayer for a Blessed Union

Blessed God, bless our unions and fill them with your divine love. Grant us an ever-flowing stream of your Big Blessed Love. May all people living with mental illness experience your blessing and love forever and ever. Amen.

Epilogue:

God's Love Never Ends

While I was writing this book, my oldest brother Scott was in a psychiatric inpatient treatment center in Jacksonville, Florida. On Good Friday he checked himself into the hospital because he was feeling suicidal, a common symptom of bipolar disorder he has struggled with for a long time. During my brother's hospitalization, I spoke to him on the phone, listening to his concerns, asking him what he wanted prayers for, and saying "I love you" as he cried his goodbye.

Today is my brother's first day out of the hospital. I know there will probably be many days to come that feel for me like his first day out—the precariousness, the need to always have something prepared to say, if not to him (I know I can't "talk him down" from suicidal thoughts) then to our mom, our other siblings. He's better. Or, he's gone. I was there on his wedding day and on the day when his wife called and over the phone told him she wanted a divorce because the weight of his chronic, serious mental illness was too much.

I often feel helpless in the face of chronic and serious mental illness because there is nothing I can do to make the mental illness go away from the people I love. So, I listen. I whisper a prayer. I light a candle. I write. I break the silence about mental illness because so many of us are crying silent tears in its shadows. We are in inpatient treatment centers, we are in prison cells, we are in executive suites, we are in classrooms, and we are in churches. We carry mental illness wherever we go, including into our relationships with those we love. There is no shame in living with a mental illness. We are in good company. God is with us. Mental illness cannot separate us from the love of God.

1 Corinthians 13 is often read at wedding ceremonies because the scripture promises love gets first place. Greater than faith and hope, love is what lasts because love never ends. I have read this scripture passage dozens of times. At first, I understood it primarily in the context of contemporary marriage, because that is where we so often place it.

Then one year, my congregation chose to study and interpret this passage from a different perspective. Instead of thinking about 1 Corinthians 13 through the frame of a newlywed couple's love for each other, we thought about it as God's unconditional love for each one of us. And we realized that when God is the lover, love becomes even more powerful than we can imagine.

Many blessed unions don't last forever. But does that mean God's love for us has ended? No. What mental illness has taught me is that God's love never ends. And this is my source of hope: in the midst of mental illness there is divine healing and Big Blessed Love.

Sometimes love is a whisper. Sometimes love is a cry. Sometimes love is a prayer. Sometimes love holds us tight. Sometimes love lets us go. God's love for us never ends. The Big Blessed Love is forever.

Acknowledgements

I offer my deepest gratitude to all the people who embraced my first book *Blessed Are the Crazy: Breaking the Silence About Mental Illness, Family, and Church*. Thank you to my readers for encouraging me to continue to tell the true stories that heal us. Thank you for blessing me in the creation of this next book that breaks the silence about our most intimate partnerships. Thank you to Chalice Press for saying "I do" all over again since our first *Blessed* book together.

Thank you to Beth and David Booram for their hospitality and for providing sacred space to write at Fall Creek Abbey in Indianapolis. Thank you to Susan Herman for our friendship since freshman year at Trinity University and editing wisdom. Thank you to my circle of support of early readers who graciously offered valuable feedback to make this book better: Mark Briley, Aleze Fulbright, Jill Howard, Rachael Keefe, Caleb Lines, and Kim Gage Ryan. Thank you to my partners in ministry at First Congregational United Church of Christ in Indianapolis and my colleagues in the national staff of the United Church of Christ. Thank you to our circle of friends and for the therapeutic and mental health support provided by CenterPoint Counseling, a ministry of Second Presbyterian Church of Indianapolis.

Thank you to my late maternal grandparents who opened their home and hearts to my mother and the five of us children, saving our lives. Thank you to my late father whose terminal struggle with serious mental illness inspired my vocational journey towards breaking the silence about mental illness in search of healing. Thank you to my mom, for believing in me and loving me, always. Thank you to Jonathan who works with me every day to build a more blessed union. Finally, thank you God for endless big blessed love.

Blessed Union Journal

Chapter 1: Breaking the Silence

When you think about being part of the movement to break the silence about mental illness and marriage, what are three things you think are important to say? What do you wish other people knew about mental illness and marriage?

Chapter 2: Mental Health Justice in the Blessed Union

How do you experience mental health as a justice issue? What would "doing justice, loving kindness and walking humbly" (Micah 6:8) look like in your marriage? What are three things you can do to work towards mental health justice?

_____

_____

_____

_____

_____

_____

_____

_____

_____

_____

_____

_____

_____

_____

_____

_____

_____

_____

_____

_____

Chapter 3: Do You Promise

How does mental illness (in you or your partner or both) impact your marriage? What is the most challenging aspect? What would you say to yourself if you could go back in time to your engagement? What's the most important promise that you made in your marriage and why? If you still have them, write your original marriage vows here.

Chapter 4: To Love

What does it mean to love yourself? What does it mean to love your partner? How do you most feel loved by your partner? In what new or different ways do you wish your partner showed you love? During times of mental illness, how can you remember and hold onto this love?

Chapter 5: To Comfort

When you are experiencing a rough time with your mental health, what brings you the most comfort? How do you experience your marriage as a place of comfort? What supports outside of your marriage bring you comfort? If you could make your marriage a shelter from the storms of mental illness, what would you want to add, take away, or change about your marriage?

Chapter 8: To Be Faithful

How have you experienced God's faithfulness in your marriage? How do you feel like you are being faithful to your partner? What about mental illness makes being faithful in marriage challenging? What needs to change in order for your sense of faithfulness to be renewed or energized?

Chapter 9: As Long As You Both Shall Live

If love is the greatest part of our blessed union, what does love in marriage look like to you? What's the greatest part of your blessed union? Make a list of the three things about your marriage for which you are thankful. What's the hardest part of your marriage? Write down what's hard and ask God to help. What needs to change and what needs to stay the same in order for your blessed union to be filled with love?

Chapter 10: Blessed Union

Where do you see God's Big Blessed Love showing up in your blessed union? What is one thing you wish your partner knew about your mental health challenges? In the face of these challenges, where do you find hope for your blessed union? What changes do you need to make in your marriage relationship so that you can both live happily ever after? Write a love letter to your partner and quote your favorite line from your marriage vows.

Chapter 11: Final Thoughts

You can rewrite your own story of your blessed union. As a gift to your marriage, you are invited to create your own unique blessing. Words like "We are filled with God's Big Blessed Love" and "We can make it together one day at a time," can inspire you to keep going even when married life gets hard and overwhelming. Close your eyes and think of a few phrases that come to mind as words of blessing for your marriage. Write them down and keep them close to your heart.

Resources

Faith Resources

American Psychiatric Association Foundation, *Mental Health: A Guide for Faith Leaders.* https://www.psychiatry.org/psychiatrists/cultural-competency/faith-community-partnership

David Finnegan-Hosey, *Christ on the Psych Ward* (New York: Church Publishing, 2018).

Monica Coleman, *Bipolar Faith* (Fortress Press, 2016).

Pathways to Promise www.pathways2promise.org

Rachael A. Keefe, *The Lifesaving Church: Faith Communities and Suicide Prevention* (St. Louis: Chalice Press, 2018).

Sarah Griffith Lund, *Blessed are the Crazy: Breaking the Silence About Mental Illness, Family and Church* (St. Louis: Chalice Press, 2014).

United Church of Christ Mental Health Network www.mhn-ucc.org

Marriage Resources

Barton Goldsmith, *The Happy Couple: How to Make Happiness a Habit One Little Loving Thing at a Time* (Oakland: New Harbinger Publications. 2013).

Gary Chapman, *The Five Love Languages: The Secret to Love That Lasts* (Chicago: Northfield Publishing, 2010).

Harville Hendrix and Helen LaKelly Hunt, *Getting the Love You Want: A Guide for Couples* (New York: Henry Holt and Co., 2007).

Harville Hendrix and Helen LaKelly Hunt, *Making Marriage Simple: 10 Relationship Saving Truths* (New York: Harmony Books, 2013).

Resources for Mental Health

Linda Meyer, "After 5 Suicide Attempts, This Action Plan Helps Me Control the Chaos." December 10, 2018. *O: The Oprah Magazine.*

Mark Lukach, *My Lovely Wife in the Psych Ward: A Memoir* (New York: Harper Wave, 2017).

Mayo Clinic www.mayoclinic.org/diseases-conditions/mental-illness/symptoms-causes/syc-20374968

Mental Health America www.mentalhealthamerica.net

Mental Health Fist Aid www.mentalhealthfirstaid.org

National Alliance on Mental Illness www.nami.org

National Institute of Mental Health www.nimh.nih.gov

National Suicide Prevention Lifeline Call 1-800-273-8255 www.suicidepreventionlifeline.org

Special TIME Edition: Mental Health, a New Understanding (July 26, 2019)

WRAP Wellness, Recovery, Action Plan www.mentalhealthrecovery.com

Endnotes

1 https://bit.ly/2SxyL1x

2 https://bit.ly/2FazPp2

3 https://bit.ly/2FazPp2

4 https://bit.ly/34riMrk

5 https://bit.ly/34riMrk

6 https://bit.ly/3jxVvdA

7 https://bit.ly/3jDU39I

8 https://trinitychicago.org

9 https://bit.ly/3jxVUg6

10 https://bbc.in/2I3xlKe

11 https://bit.ly/2SvWjDN

12 https://stanford.io/2Fd1buM

13 https://bit.ly/2I7nxPv

14 https://to.pbs.org/3d3tDeQ

15 https://to.pbs.org/3d3tDeQ

16 https://bit.ly/30EjyQJ

17 https://bit.ly/2I5gCpR

18 https://bit.ly/3iCIjD1

19 https://bit.ly/3d3IeqK

20 https://bit.ly/3d3IeqK

21 https://bit.ly/34unXqx

22 https://bit.ly/30HYY1P

23 https://bit.ly/3d7e2eA

24 https://bit.ly/3iCIjD1